Sol Journeys

Alicia Wright

Editor: Nancy Kurtz

Cover Design: Meg Stewart

Cover Format: Sarah Finocchio
www.pipedreammoab.com

Author Photo: Alf Randell

Interior Format: Debora Lewis
arenapublishing.org

ISBN-13: 978-1530671427
ISBN-10: 1530671426

Contents

An Introduction

Welcome to Sol Journeys!

This series of visualizations facilitates deeper exploration into the constructs that compose the self and stimulates contemplation and internal reflection so that we may serve the greatest good for all. If the mind is a collection of belief systems, can you let go and shift beyond labels? What is your current experience? How are you benefiting the whole? I encourage each of you to question what you know, free your mind, and become fluid with your perspective.

The power of visualization and meditation are forces of nature. In order for this work to penetrate habitual belief, it is paramount to engage the focus of the brain. If you can see an object or movement in your mind, you can co-create it into your tangible reality. Do not be discouraged if you cannot perceive or sense an essence of a journey. With time and repetition, the pathways become clearer to experience new states of being. An open mind and a willingness to explore new territory are the necessary ingredients to voyage through Sol Journeys.

This manual is not meant to be read straight through, nor is it the only way to master the self. There are many roads that lead to your center. My personal journey truly began with my recovery from self-sabotaging behaviors and addictions. It is through sobriety that Sol Journeys was born. I do not profess to know the way or all the answers as I am on this journey of life with you. Sol Journeys will take you out of your comfort zone; it is through this discomfort you discover where your greatest strengths lie.

Enjoy each adventure as written; my suggestion is to record them in your own voice to fully experience the guided visualizations. Take as long as you would like to pause and integrate the scene before you during the meditations. At times, gender is assigned to guides for literary purposes. Please feel free to switch gender to suit your vision as needed. You may also choose to combine the meditations in a way that works best to make the journey yours.

Some journeys can be daily rituals; others may be only for special occasions. I do recommend exploring each Sol Journey several times to receive all of the information that is awaiting you. There is no summit to reach or end in sight; it is through each step along the way that you may find what you have been seeking. Trust your own instincts and your own path.

My intention for writing this manual is to encourage those ready to: turn their gaze inward, persevere through the dark night of the soul, liberate from the shackles of "illusive freedom", access power within, and carry a torch to illuminate the path for others to find their own treasure. We each get to decide who we are in this moment and explore which parts of the path work for us. The path is always new and creating, we along with it. May Sol Journeys encourage expansive vision and open the door to question what is possible. Enjoy the journey...

With love and gratitude,

Alicia

Notes:

A Personal Journey

An Invocation to the Great Mother

I heed your call oh Great Mother of all that is.

I am at your service.

I am here to embody and inspire your divine essence and vibration on our plane at this time.

I bear your torch and know that I will be divinely guided where, when, and with whom I am to align on this journey.

My eyes are wide open as I witness the expansion of the internal world within the temple of my heart.

My faith and compassion lead me to trust the process of this unfolding.

I know I am fully protected and supported by your generosity on all levels as one of your devoted daughters.

I bring knowledge from the depths of self-discovery to the surface; may it assist men and women to reclaim their power.

May my truth be heard by those ready to receive and may it stir the seed for those ready to awaken to a new reality.

Great Mother, I am an ambassador of your gifts.

I am your vessel and womb to create a new vision of unity and anchor it into the earth.

I am dedicated and have the endurance to withstand the test of time. I am blessed to be your conduit and fully activated!

I will dance joyously, ride the waves with style and grace, and beat the cosmic drum to the rhythm of my heart.

May I be the breath of your spirit.

I bow in deep gratitude

Namaste

A

Into the Void

I have held on to the edge of everything I have known to be true about myself and the constructs that keep order, as if my life depended on it. I have tended to all of my ducks, lined them up in a row, orchestrated their extraordinary performance, and projected to "keep it all together". Oh no! I feel myself slipping and losing my grip, no longer able to hold on to the illusive dream. Terrified of the unknown, I scream in horror without abandon as all of my comforts are removed. I am falling into a deep dark chasm with nothing to hold onto or a way to stop the accelerated momentum, down, down, down, spinning into the abyss. An echo of Alice in Wonderland, the question: "Who am I?" comes to the forefront of this quest and serves as a road map winding deep into the corners of myself. As layers upon layers are stripped away and I let go of what no longer serves me, I dive deep into the pools of self-discovery.

****

In the void there is only emptiness, darkness, stillness, and silence. This place of isolation has no structure, identity or sense of belonging. There is nothing. No one to see, nothing to be, no projects to complete—only an empty vessel. In this voided landscape nothing is stable and there are no guarantees. This zero vantage point can be a raw and unsettling place, yet a deep well of power. This is the place where creation begins; this is where we discover the clear channels of intuition and inspiration. What lies on the other side of this black hole within us? Only those who have the courage to face what lies beyond perception and the strength of personal resolve may enter here. Every fiber of our being will be tested, stretching beyond all limitations, without the promise of a secure platform or outcome. It is humbling to fully accept this place of the unknown, and to allow the mystery to unfold without our personal agendas attached. The torch in the darkness tells us that every transformation builds inner strength and that what doesn't kill us only makes us stronger!

Most of us run from this place of quiet introspection like the plague and fill our spaces with endless social engagements, activities, to do lists, old story lines, and grandiose plans for the future. This chatter props us up and creates distraction that diverts our attention from what lies beyond action, beyond the container, the machine, and the rat race. The emptiness of the void is not something you can run away from. Bob Marley said it best: "Ya running and ya runnin and ya running away, but ya can't run away from yaself. Ya must have done something wrong, why can't ya find the place where ya belong?" The truth is: It doesn't matter where you go, there you are!

What if we leaned into the jagged edges of what is unfamiliar, uncomfortable and uncertain, and bravely faced the abyss with no foundation or hand holds? What if instead of losing our minds to our insecurities, fears and doubts, we held space, loosened our grip, and stood with open arms to life? What if we stopped trying to figure everything out, rationalizing, compartmentalizing, analyzing, and debating everything we know, feel, and believe to be true? What if we didn't have to prove anything to anyone, or needed reward or recognition for our deeds? What if we could let go of who we strive to be or who we have become? What if we dropped our stories, our ribbons, our badges, and our scars of life?

Some of us will never admit that we need approval or acceptance from the outside in order to feel okay in our own skins, while others wear this insecurity like a security blanket. If we are not being productive, helping someone, or saving the world, do we feel worthy? We tend to cling tightly to circumstances, relationships, and social status; we lock our jaws, hold our breath and death-grip life and love with such fierce desire. In the process, we restrict the flow and become unable to receive the omnipresent gifts of the moment. It is how we handle this space without definition that defines our character.

Loosening our grip means we let go of the details and know that everything will work out in due time. The perception of impaired forward momentum can be frustrating and disappointing; yet when we recognize this as part of the process, we do not have to identify with the obstacles that present themselves. Learning endurance, tolerance, and maintaining composure in spite of delays and difficulties assist in our maturity.

When we understand that part of our neurosis is a product of our perceived separation from Source and part of it is learned social conditioning, we begin to open to the healing of our dis-ease. When we realize that we are not alone or even in the driver's seat, there is an ability to release our resistances and struggles. It is refreshing to remember that everything happens for a reason and that it's all part of the divine plan unfolding into perfection; there is no need to fight it, push it, or hurry it along. May we begin to look at life as a sacred journey, and know the universe has our back.

Be present, calm, and centered. Breathe deeply; create a sacred space and morning ritual that includes introspection, time to receive divine guidance, and invoke the intention for compassion and gratitude with every interaction for the day. Just like any habit, we have to pluck what no longer serves us out of our lives, and then become vigilant with our affirmations and intentions to create new pathways of action and response. Notice when we get derailed. What are the triggers, the time, the place, and the circumstance that take us out of our original peaceful loving state? This is a daily practice, a lifetime journey. The learning never ends as we continue to acknowledge and notice how we filter our experiences and justify our actions. There is no such thing as mastery of the human experience. In our goal oriented society, it is not how fast we make it to the end or achieve our goals; our happiness and success are measured by each step along the way. With faith and acceptance of our growth, may we learn to embody grace.

When we slow down and dissolve into the void, we raise our vibration, assist in our personal evolution and become a part of the true revolution of awakening! We experience a deep knowingness of the universal mind, feeling of oneness, deep peace of restoration, guidance of intuition, discovery of our unique gifts, clarity of vision and voice, clearing of karmic debts and toxins, and euphoria of pure bliss. When there is a change of reference points in one's self, reality has to shift to support this new understanding. This is how we serve humanity and invite the world to become a better place. When we claim our excellence, we inspire and give others permission to do the same. The more we can sit within our own skin and rejoice in our unique expressions without distraction, the more we can move mountains and create social, political, global, and cosmic change.

When we know the truth of emptiness, there is nothing that can stand in our way, no obstacle too insurmountable to overcome. It starts by declaring ENOUGH, stop the madness, stop running away from ourselves. Let us stand firm, dance, and raise our voices in song and praise. We are no longer victims of circumstance or creatures of habit. Let us break the mold and become co-creators of this miracle of life. This is a new era, a paradigm shift, a beginning of a new way of relating to ourselves and the world around us. Let us surrender into the void and practice loving ourselves more. This is our purpose of re-remembering our greatness and accessing our multi-dimensional capabilities. Welcome and drink deeply from the restorative essence of divine balance, peace and unconditional love. Enjoy and play in these new landscapes without the shackles of predestined roles, duties, or karma. Let us be honest with ourselves as we answer: "Who am I?" Where does the rabbit hole lead? Let go, without expectation, judgment, or definition, and experience true freedom. This is the power of embracing the gifts from the shadows and the depths of the void.

****

I sit on the edge of the void no longer afraid of what the abyss has in store for me. I have been to the depths of the void and been reborn. I no longer run from the unknowable. I remain present for the direction and guidance I am given. The divine flow is the wind beneath me and I need not resist or struggle against it. I am not who I once was, I remain open for what will be, enjoying the unfolding discovery of my true self. I now know faith, acceptance, and grace and choose to embody them through life's chaotic spells. I am peace. I am love. I am golden light. I am hope. I am a humble servant to humanity. I am here now. I fly Free. Blessed be the transformational chasms of the void!

Notes:

The Battle of the Addict

The art of removing denial and the need to fill the Void

I have been sober since February 28th 2011, and I have begun to see reality in a new way. I used to live a self-serving existence, a slave to substances to get me into a mellow and perceived connected state of mind. There always seemed to be a reason to celebrate, a justified indulgence, and then getting high quietly became a daily habit. When I was alone doing mundane house work, going for a hike, or heading to the store, my habit became my trusted companion and I became socially accepted and invincible. I knew deep down inside myself that this routine was sabotaging the core of who I was. I was tormented for years trying to quit and failing.

What helped me change my life was a group of friends who pointed out that I was a liar and a fake if I continued to seek the easy way out—the path of an addict. It was hard to hear, yet it was true and I knew it. I chose to no longer be a victim of social conditioning and was willing to walk the path of sobriety. The challenge was on to prove to myself, to my friends and family, and the world that I could do it.

Addicts, much like politicians, are experts at the art of deception and self-justification. They are entwined in habit. Smoke this, eat that, snort this, toke that, slam this, shoot that; intoxication and experiencing the feeling of euphoria has been an integral part of the human experience from the beginning of time. Society supports the notion of instant gratification, excessive gluttony, and indulgences of drinking and drugging at most social gatherings. Family and friends also influence and perpetuate this recreational addictive behavior, accept it as normal, and encourage any reason to celebrate.

Whether intoxication is present at sport games, music events, the weekend, a birthday party, on vacations, or out of sheer boredom, it eventually becomes a daily quest. Whether your vice is beer, shopping, adrenaline, marijuana, food, sex, sweets, cocaine, Xanax, heroin, caffeine, money, ambition, exercise or Diet Pepsi, feeding the insatiable appetite is always the same. Anything that you need to consume daily to maintain your "mental health" is a dependency. Addiction comes in many forms and will rear its ugly head around every corner, robbing us of our power and internal conviction.

The latest and greatest high/buzz, altering one's state of mind, is big business. Think about how many people you know who are dependent on pharmaceuticals. A pill promises to numb out the pain, the discomfort, the sadness and the darkness. This is a false and empty endeavor; filling the void with substances will never be enough. Our instinct is to run away from the pit within ourselves. The darkness can be overwhelming, all encompassing, debilitating and un-fun. Instead of embracing "down time" and using the void as our muse for creative expression, we continue to prop ourselves up for fear of falling apart. It takes a lot of strength, will power, and self-love to sit in the pit, look in the mirror, and begin the search for truth. Nothing good comes from using; there are countless tales of woe. We end up on the edge of our sanity. Facing ourselves at the end of the day is the bottom line.

When life begins to come apart at the seams, leading you to rock bottom, instead of avoiding your pain, the best advice I have is to detach, observe the monkey mind of the ego, and sit with it as long as it takes. Healing takes place when we begin to identify the core of the unease, habit, and abuse. It is important to go to the root of the addiction for it is easy to exchange one habit for another. Asking why, how did we get here, where did the unhealthy behaviors come from, are actions that lead to sobriety. Establishing new healthy rituals and routines to replace the unhealthy response to external discomfort is an essential piece of the healing process.

Finding support groups and other healing teams to assist in unraveling addiction from your life can also be
helpful. Homeostasis may not have been a part of your
life for quite some time; learning how to live without
your vice may feel like learning how to walk again. Re-
balancing and finding steady ground to build a new
foundation are the victories of a rejuvenated, inspired
life.

My strength now comes from saying "I'm good" when
someone offers their vice rather than accepting the
invitation of oblivion. The sober life can be perceived as
a lonely road; at times it is. Walking the path of an
outcast, counter to the masses, takes the spirit of a
warrior. But many people envy the freeing of self-denial
and want to know how it is possible. One step at a time,
one day at a time. The challenges are daily, yet the
rewards are many and worth every bit of discomfort.
Change can be difficult—why repeat the endless cycles
of the quit/binge torture only to be left wounded, torn,
frayed, disgusted, battered and broken? Substance
dependency is a self-inflicted prison in which the key
for the shackles we place on ourselves can only be found
within. It has been a dedicated practice that I do not take
lightly. Being a clear channel, being present and
available in my life are the most important truths to me;
it will never be worth compromising for any high. I

choose freedom from addiction and continue to dream big!

Note: This path may not be for everyone. If you have a medical condition, follow your doctor's orders.

Notes:

Inspiration for Daily Practice

Aligning with the Ancient Rhythm

This ritual is designed to humbly mark your place within the great cycles of life, assign an entry and exit point within the circle, create pillars for each direction to invoke your sacred space, and honor the myriad forces present for creation and your existence within it. This ritual can be practiced daily at sunrise or sunset, before ceremonies, at sacred sites, before prayer and contemplation, or at any time you wish to get back to your center.

Note: There are many tribes who honor the directions and elements in their unique traditional way. I have much respect for them all. This ritual is a combination of native and pantheistic influences. It is a guideline and not intended to be the only way to access this wisdom. You may decide to be barefoot and wear ceremonial garb such as a head wrap, cape, or scarf that is special for this purpose. Use what works best for you.

Before you begin, connect with benevolent, unconditional, and creative forces of love—create a sacred space.

[1] Breathe deeply into your center and this will help you feel fully present in this moment.

Face the Sun. Bow to the golden orb that gives life and connects you with the cosmic cycles. Raise your hands up to the sky, receive the warmth and solar codes into your being, and feel your hands charge with light. Bring them to your heart and pat your chest four times as you rededicate the solar infusion into your presence. Feel your connection to the sun. Lift your hands back to the sun and then smudge them over your body from head to toe four times, each time grounding the energy into Earth. This clears any debris impeding your connection to Source and prevents lower frequencies from entering your sacred space. You are now a clear channel and solar powered! (This ceremony can also be applied to moonlight and lunar codes received on the full and new moon.)

Face the East. Bow to the East, the direction of illumination, rebirth and initiation; allow yourself to be uplifted through your inner vision and spiritual infusion. Traditionally the East is the symbol for the rising sun. It is also the home of living color, the time of spring, the epoch of the child (maiden), and represents

---

[1] Refer to Protective Shield Activation on page 33

the element of fire. This is the direction where you determine your focus, plant the seeds of your intentions, and ignite your faith. Honor the essence of this direction—it gives you purpose, propels you on your journey, and reflects the communion with Spirit. Receive the wisdom of the East and set the pillar within your sacred circle.

Contemplation: How does this direction affect your life? What is your vision? How will this leap of faith carry you forward on your journey?

Face the South. Bow to the South, the direction of giving, growth, trust and movement. Step into the waters of giving energy motion often understood as emotions. Traditionally this direction is the home of the plant kingdom, the time of summer, the epoch of the adult (mother), and represents the element of water. The South is where passion pulses through your creative expression, where you tend to that which you have planted, learn your place within family and community, and harness vigilant focus. Honor the essence of this direction as you co-create with commitment and endurance and release expectation of the outcome. Receive the wisdom of the South and set the pillar within your sacred circle.

Contemplation: How does this direction affect your life? How do you nurture your vision? What emotions come to the surface?

Face the West. Bow to the West, the direction of the physical transformation of your intention; harvest and receive the gifts of manifestation. Traditionally the West is the home of the mineral kingdom, the time of fall, the epoch of the elder (crone), and the element of earth. Honor the essence of this direction as the holder of knowledge—the keeper of genetic codes. This is the direction of reaping what you have sown, sharing your bounty in celebration, and letting go of what you have created. Receive the wisdom of the West and set the pillar within our sacred circle.

Contemplation: How does this direction affect your life? What are the gifts of your vision? How does it feel to hold what you have created then set it free?

Face the North. Bow to the North, the direction of the mystery; surrender into stillness through the shadows of hibernation and receive guidance. Traditionally the North is the home of the animal kingdom, the time of winter, the epoch of death (rebirth), and represents the element of air. This is the direction of contraction, rest, and healing; a place to connect and listen to Spirit, receive inspired messages through dreamtime as well as digest and integrate this wisdom. Honor the mental essence of this direction with strength and courage as intuition and introspection arrive within the dark cave of your transformation. Receive the wisdom of the North and set the pillar within your sacred circle.

Contemplation: How does this direction affect your life? What do you hear in the silence within? How do you feel in the void?

<u>Lift your hands to the Sky.</u> Feel your connection to the bigger picture, the cosmos, and the unseen realms. There is much more than meets the eye and you are a part of it. Honor the higher power in its full essence as the Creator of this world. Honor the ancestors, the guardians, the spirit guides, the energetic realms, your soul family, and your personal team. As you look to the sky and watch the clouds swirl with the hands of fate, see it carry the torrents of change within its billows, claim your place in the ether. Your full participation permits you to become part of the celestial rhythm as the stars proceed within the galactic spin. As you lower your hands, you become a conduit between Heaven and Earth.

<u>Place your hands upon the Earth.</u> Feel your Mother and nurture her with your fully activated presence. Bow in respect for all you receive unconditionally and ground into her balanced vibration. Earth not only sustains you with her plethora of nutrients in all forms, she gifts you with shelter and a place to interact with fellow creators as you travel. Everything comes from Earth as everything must return, and you are not an exception. As you place your hands upon the earth's back, feel her heart beat, rest in gratitude. You are blessed to be a child of Earth and have chosen to be here at this time.

Dedicate your Step. State what you would like to manifest for the whole. The power of speaking your intention, prayer and focus aligns you to your purpose and mission throughout your day. This statement becomes your act of service and attracts who and what you need to actualize it.

Contemplation: What do you choose to bring forth at this time?

Now, since you have purified yourself, set up pillars for the directions within, and dedicated your inspired presence in each step upon the earth; turn clockwise four times to honor all of creation and verbalize part of the traditional Navajo Beauty Way song:

"I walk with beauty all around me, as I walk the beauty way. I walk with beauty before me. I walk with beauty behind me. I walk with beauty above me. I walk with beauty below me. I walk with beauty all around me, as I walk the beauty way."

When you finish this invocation, you have fully claimed your place within the sacred hoop of life. This is a great time to voice prayers from your heart space for the whole. Give thanks to each direction for any insights gained. Honor the space you have created, close the circle, and let the energy flow back into the earth.

A traditional ceremonial closing: "The circle is open, and yet unbroken. May the love of Spirit be ever in your heart. Merry meet and merry part. And merry meet again. Blessed Be."

When you practice this ritual you create a vortex of manifestation, balance within your center, pillars of protection, and a platform of support. May your words, actions, and connections be blessings to uplift the collective as you fulfill your purpose with an overflowing cup.

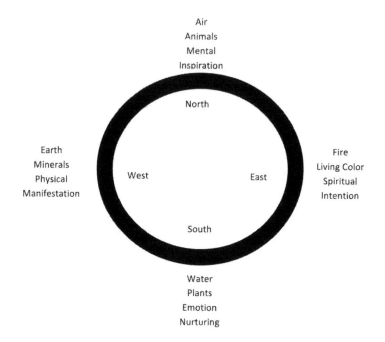

Air
Animals
Mental
Inspiration

North

Earth
Minerals
Physical
Manifestation

West

East

Fire
Living Color
Spiritual
Intention

South

Water
Plants
Emotion
Nurturing

Protective Shield Activation

Before any ritual or journey create a sacred space.

Set the tone: "I create a sacred space of benevolent, unconditional and creative love." Visualize yourself inside a golden grid. Extend the channels of the grid in all directions of energy flow and expansion. This creates a level of protection from lower vibration and entities when working in the energetic and ethereal realms.

Dr. Nancy R. Harris, DSS, Professional Intuitive and Psychotherapist, taught me much of the following ritual derived from *The Rainbow Shield Technique*. According to her teachings, "When we connect via visualization to all the colors in the spectrum and to all the kingdoms, we are reminding ourselves that we are a part of the All and due to this connection we are always protected."

When we shine bright we may attract all types of energy, including darkness. In order to remain in communion with our Source and not have to defend nor defeat our adversaries, invoke sacred space. For more protection before uneasy encounters, astral traveling, or daily living for sensitive people, create the Rainbow Shield.

During this exercise, imagine the shield coming from your heart center and expanding in concentric circles throughout your body until you are fully encompassed by a spectrum of color. Then, continue to create your sacred space with the kingdoms and elements as guided.

1. Call on your guides and ancestors of your greatest good to join you.

2. Place a pillar in each of the directions to anchor you into the moment.

3. Wrap yourself in purple light as if it were a cloak. Put a purple flame over your heart to guard your inner heart space. This is the last resort should anything get past all the other layers of your shield.

4. Visualize a bubble or shield of blue light around the trunk of your body over the purple flame.

5. Expand a green light around your elbows, knees, and neck over the blue layer.

6. Then, place a yellow light around your forearms, shins, and mouth over the green layer.

7. Visualize an orange light around your wrists, ankles, and eyes over the yellow layer.

8. Then imagine a red light around the center of your palms, feet, and top of head over the orange layer.

9. Envelop yourself completely at least six inches past hands, below feet, and above head in a pastel color around the red layer.

10. Then, call in an insect family (bees, lady bugs, butterflies, etc.) to surround your shield.

11. Next, cover your shield with flowers of your choice.

12. Envision a tree in your sacred space to lean your back up against.

13. Place a stone, crystal, or wand in your hand.

14. Ask a bird to join you.

15. Call a forest animal to enter your rainbow shield.

16. Ask a mammal of the sea to join you within your sacred space.

17. Then, call to four animals who attack if attacked (i.e. scorpions, snakes, tigers, lions, bears, badgers). Surround yourself with these protectors, one to the right, left, front and back of you. You no longer have to fight as they will do what they must to protect you.

18. Now you have the support of the animal, plant and mineral kingdoms; place a pyramid of any color over

the top of your body. Visualize the apex one foot above your head and the base one foot below the base of your spine. Sit within this pyramid with all that you have called into your space and be energized.

19. Then, choose an element to surround the pyramid — a ring of fire, earth, water, or air as your first layer of defense.

20. Connect to the Source from the top of your head through the top of the pyramid and ground to the core of the earth from the base of your spine through the base of the pyramid. Take as many breaths as you would like in this expanded state. When you are ready, draw the connection of these two points into the center of your heart.

21. Create a dedication or intention for the energy cultivated. For example: May I be a conduit of the greatest good for all and serve to the best of my ability.

You are now shielded and have created a sacred space that only those invited may enter. With practice, you will be able to invoke your shield in a matter of seconds. When you have gained this level of security you will create a greater connection with Source and be inspired. Move forward, not in fear but in confidence that you are protected by the powers that be. Live from your heart; may it lead the way!

Practice: What does your shield look like? Draw all of the layers of your Rainbow Shield to enhance this visualization.

Notes:

Connecting to Source

This meditation of internal circuitry and alignment with energy flow can be practiced in its entirety or each part separately. It is best to understand, pause, and experience each circuit before continuing to the next. For some, a week is a good amount of time to become comfortable; for others, a day will do. Repetition facilitates a stronger circuit and helps activate personal responsibility. A daily practice is recommended.

Note: The concept of grounding and connecting to a higher power may be different for everyone. This may also change with time and perspective. Please use what works best for you in the moment as this is one possibility of many. Feeling connected to your center, regardless of your surroundings, is the underlying purpose of this meditation.

Before you begin: Create a sacred space of benevolent, creative, unconditional love. Surround yourself with a golden grid.

Part 1: Internal circuit

Focus your attention on the central channel inside the spine called the pranic tube. Visualize energy (it could be a ball of light, a color, a sound, a vibration or whatever works for you) traveling up one side of your central channel on the inhale (from the base of your spine to the top of your head) and exhale your attention down the other side. You can also imagine the chakras (the seven energy centers within your body) as wheels that spin clockwise as your breath goes by. Feel the sensation of energy flowing through your internal circuit. Repeat this cycle of attention with your breath for as long as you would like. (Pause). This practice focuses the mind, creates awareness of your internal energy circuit, and strengthens the concept of "centering" within.

Part 2: Connecting to the core of the earth

Note: The core perspective is pure speculation. Some choose to ground into their hearts instead. If other labels or vantage points work better for you, please feel free to interject your version of grounding.

Visualize the core of the earth as a giant geode that acts as a recycling station for the two extremes of stagnant energy and excess energy. To ground your circuit into the core, visualize copper lines or roots either from the base of your spine or from the center of your feet, and effortlessly follow your attention through the surface of the earth down through all of her layers to the center. Once the connection is made, hook your grounding rods into the core. Now, breathe and connect your internal circuit to the core of the earth. (Breathe from the base of your spine up your central channel and when you exhale, follow your attention to the core. Inhale from the core up through your spine to the top of your head.)

Exhale what no longer serves you out of your body to the core visualizing a dark color; and breathe clean, clear, revitalized energy back into your body. Take several breaths with this focus and feel the sensation of energy flowing through the circuit. (Pause). This practice has the ability to ground energy, calm anxiety, treat depression or illness, and bring your attention into the present moment. When your energy is purified, you can also use this practice as a way to give back to the earth.

Part 3: Connecting to the center of the cosmos

Note: The cosmic perspective is pure speculation. If Creator, Great Spirit, God, Goddess, Divine, Central Sun or other labels work better for you, please feel free to interject your version of your higher power.

To expand your circuit and tap into the center of the cosmos, visualize an energetic line extending from the crown of your head, directly above you to the brilliance of Source. Now, connect your internal circuit to this vibrant celestial realm. (Breathe from the base of your spine up your central channel, through the top of your head connecting to your cosmic center. When you exhale, follow your attention back to the base of your spine.) Continue this loop for several breaths and feel the sensation of energy flowing through the circuit. (Pause). This practice will expand your awareness outside of the human ego, connect you to divine presence, create an opening to inspired thought, and facilitate your ability to receive messages from your higher self, ancestors, and other beings of benevolent, unconditional, creative love.

Part 4: Becoming a conduit

In your mind's eye, run the energy from the core of the earth through your central channel to the center of the cosmos. Visualize a big circuit connecting these two points with your breath, you melting within it. You may also visualize a vertical figure 8 crossing through the major centers of your body—your solar plexus or your heart. Take several breaths with this focus and feel the sensation of energy flowing through this connection. (Pause). Running energy between these power poles will tap you into the energy available all around us. When you become a channel between Heaven and

Earth, you claim your empowered, co-creative, and multi-dimensional self. At any point in the day when you begin to feel tired, anxious, or overwhelmed, you can reconnect and run this energy through your spine!

Part 5: Infinite expansion

After a connection to Source is made, expand yourself slowly and limitlessly in all directions. In this way, you can become one with everything and be nothing at the same time. Enjoy your full expansion for as long as you wish. (Pause). When you are ready, begin to collect your energy and bring it back inside. Place the combination of the cosmos and the earth into your heart or solar plexus. Feel a deep sense of peace and expansion inside your body activating your inner power. This vibration affects everyone around you which also enhances and serves humanity as a whole.

Through connecting to Source you may receive inspiration and dreams, notice synchronicity, access a dimensional viewpoint, feel vibration between people, channel healing energy through you, and experience a greater sense of self.

Notes:

Creating a Pathway

Meeting your Team

Breathe deeply and center yourself. Imagine yourself in the jungle. Use all of your senses to bring yourself completely to this place. What do you hear? What do you see? What do you smell? What do you taste? What do you feel? You find yourself with a group of people on a guided trip to experience the wealth of this ancient resource. Your tour guide announces that you will now have time to freely explore this area. When you hear the bell it will be time to reconvene and return to this location.

The group disperses in all directions. Following your intuition, you are led to a path less traveled. You see where the jungle creates an opening through overgrowth that invites you to go more deeply inside. As you travel slowly and breathe everything in, the passage is thick with life and you feel safe, melting within it. You hear water in the distance. You enter a clearing within the trees. Beyond the reeds you see a hidden pool. You are mesmerized by the crystal clear blue water and the ability to see into the depths of its bottom. There is also a spectacular waterfall to the far side of the oasis pixelating rainbows within its spray. You sit in awe of this natural treasure and commune with its epic beauty.

As you sit and observe this amazing sanctuary, you hear a stirring on the edges of your perception. There is another presence at the watering hole drinking deeply from her truth. Your eyes meet and you sense this is a kindred spirit: there is no fear, only a sense of love. Whichever animal appears to you is one of your guides. Communication within your mind crosses the norm within species and initiates telepathic resonance. Your animal guide explains beyond the spoken word, "Another spirit guide is waiting on the other side of the waterfall and you must not forget to bring an offering. You must leave everything behind when you enter the spring; you can take nothing with you, especially your conditioned mind. In order to receive the wisdom from beyond the veil, you must be willing to purify and surrender yourself to the spirit of the jungle. This journey is not for the faint of heart."

You nod in devout understanding as you prepare for the transition of the known into the unknown. Before you enter the liquid distiller, you humbly bow to your new ally. You give gratitude for the guidance you have received, and realize that your spirit animal is a gatekeeper of higher knowledge. Your animal guide relays, "I am always with you. You can consciously access my power and medicine at any time." Before your animal spirit turns and leaves her watering hole she imparts, "Be mindful when working with guides and ask if they are there for your greatest good. Not all guides appear as they are or have your best interest at heart. Beware!" With that, she is gone. You catalog her words of wisdom for later.

As you look into the pool, something shiny catches your eye. You decide that what lies there will be your offering to your second spirit guide behind the waterfall. As you dive in, the cool water enters every cell of your being. You can palpably feel a shift in your DNA as you let go of your old identity and open to all possibilities. You become nothing and you become everything. You dive deep and your treasure meets you there. Your prize in hand, you rise to the surface and fill your lungs with air.

You find yourself closer to the waterfall. To overcome its resistance, you swim faster and more vigorously than you have ever done in your life. The current is strong and unwavering, yet you persevere and penetrate the tumultuous barrier. When you finally resurface, you find yourself on the other side of the falls. The sound is all consuming, yet it echoes the stillness within you. You pull yourself out of the water and see a bench with a towel and a robe. Take a few moments to dry off and contemplate your new vantage point.

From the bench you see steps leading into a big cavern with torches lighting the way. The ambiance is inviting and you are drawn inside. You notice a little table with two chairs, a candle, a tea pot, and two cups upon it. You are invited to join the tea party. There is a profound shock of recognition and communion along with a deep sense of coming home when you see your spirit guide. Enjoy your tea. After a pause, he explains to you that he is only one of your guides and is there for your greatest good.

"You have a whole team of spirit guides, spirit animals, ancestors, guardians, and cosmic beings with the highest vibration of love to assist you," he says. "Even though we cannot always be seen on physical planes, we are with you. You are never alone. Ask and you shall receive our gifts. We communicate through the elements, through whisperings, through people, through your dreams, and sometimes through waking visions. There is much hidden from your perception. We will guide you through the illusion when you are ready and wish to see clearly. You are here on Earth at this time to learn, to forgive, to evolve and to bring forth your gift to serve the whole. You are the gift, you are the offering. When your journey is complete, you will join us within the golden grid. You are the torch for us all. We believe in you and your inspired mission. Feel all of us with you.

"Let us create a sacred space within the grid of benevolent, creative, and unconditional love. Close your eyes and open your heart in all directions. Invite your team to join you within your sacred space. Bow in honor and respect for each arrival as they take their place within your inner circle." You sit at the center of the circle. "Expand your awareness to the center of the cosmos and the core of the earth, run your circuit through your heart. Receive your team's energy flow into your center for a few breaths. Feel their support and healing surrounding you," your guide concludes.

You bow in gratitude to your team for the support and love you experienced from them. Your heart is full and singing. As they return to their spheres and your spirit guide remains before you at the table within the cavern, you reach into the pocket of your robe and pull out your treasure as an offering. Your guide accepts your gift. "Know that we are here for you whenever you ask," he reminds you. "There is much to explore when you are ready." In the distance, you hear a bell ringing. It is time for you to return. You humbly bow to your guide for the gift of sustenance and love beyond words.

You return to the bench and leave your robe for the next time. Facing the inside of the waterfall, a profound change has occurred within yourself, for you know your team is near. You enter the raging waters and let the current push you through the veil back into the jungle's embrace. You glide effortlessly through the electric blue water to the edge where your old form awaits. As you exit bliss and reclaim your material expression, you realize that even though you appear the same on the outside, you are inspired by the messages and medicine you received on your journey. You bow in deep gratitude for the gifts from the oasis within the wild. You make your way back up the path and join the rest of the group. You hear the tour guide ask: "Would anyone like to share some wisdom from the jungle?" You smile and decide for now to keep your experience to yourself.

Heart Temple Activation

Get comfortable, relax, and breathe deeply. Find yourself in your favorite special place. Use all of your senses to take in your environment. What is happening in this very moment? There is a bench on the outskirts of your space. There is someone on the bench waiting for you to join her. This guide is here for your greatest good and will assist you with this practice today. Sit down and receive the message she has for you. Give gratitude to your guide for accompanying you into the temple of your heart.

Now take a look at the path and the steps leading up to your heart temple. What condition are they in? Are they disheveled and overgrown from lack of care or are they bright and shiny? Take in the scene of your heart temple with a detached viewpoint and suspend judgment. Before you ascend the steps on your left, there is a torch burning on a long staff. She asks you to take it with you.

With the torch in your hand, you bring your full presence into each step. With slow and deliberate movements, you gain elevation. After a short while, you arrive at the opening of your heart temple. Before you enter, take a look around as you now have a new perspective of your special place below.

As you enter, your guide suggests you light the fire at the center of your heart space. When the kindling ignites, you are able to view the inside of your sanctuary. She hands you some herbs to add to the fire to purify yourself and the space around you. Your guide shows you how to smudge yourself with fan-like motions all over your body as the smoke spirals to the ceiling. With the sweet smell you feel refreshed and clear. Light the candles around your temple with the torch.

Notice an altar on the left near the door. What is there? Notice the sitting area. What does it look like? There is also a table with a tea pot and cups, as well as a cupboard full of the finest teas. Are there any sounds in the background? What is the state of the interior? Are there cracks in the walls or decorations hanging? Is it dusty or clean? What color are the walls and the cushions? Take a moment to take in your heart space.

Your guide makes you some tea and asks you to have a seat, make yourself comfortable. She explains: "You can make any improvements, rearrange, or redecorate your space effortlessly, with the focus of your mind." If you choose to make any changes, upgrade the haven of your heart at this time. Now that you are comfortable within your temple, your guide says, "It is time to venture more deeply into yourself. Invoke a sacred space of benevolent, unconditional and creative love, and connect to Source.

"While keeping this connection, bring your attention to your heart center. Start to feel your heart expand in all directions. Let the energy fill your inner heart space, expand your heart energy to fill your heart temple, expand your heart energy to fill your special place around the heart temple. Continue to expand your heart energy beyond the world of time and space until it is pixelated beyond form into the void and mystery where nothing and everything exist together. Feel the state of your heart fully expanded in all directions.

"This is the place of true compassion, unconditional love, bliss and communion with the divine. When you live with your heart wide open, and love all of creation with this full capacity, you create Paradise on Earth. This is your birthright and one of the reasons why you are here. Remember and come to your heart temple often to share this great gift," your guide says smiling.

"When you are ready, from this fully expanded state, begin to contract this energy back into your heart center. Take as much time as you need. Your heart chakra is fully activated and the electromagnetic current is flowing from within you extending outwardly to the world. Feel this flow." She concludes, "The external world is a reflection of your internal experience. We attract who we are into our lives." This gives you much to contemplate.

Bring your awareness back to the inside of your heart temple and your presence within it. Your guide lets you know that you can return here as often as you would like and recommends a daily practice. Before you leave, blow out all of the candles and visit your altar. Your guide shares the universal law of reciprocity: You receive what you give. Light a candle and add any prayers, devotions, and objects to your altar as your offering. Take another look around and fill yourself from the inner glow of this sacred space.

As you emerge from your inner landscape, look out to the horizon. Take your gaze as far as you can see and use all of your senses to notice any changes to your environment. Now is the time to fly! Become a bird of your choice and experience your special place from above, spreading out your wings on the currents of the wind. Fly far and as fast as you like, enjoying this freedom of flight. As you explore a sense of liberation in your new form, reflect on everything you are grateful for in your life. Enjoy this moment.

When you are ready, come back to your human form on the top of the steps outside of your heart temple, standing next to your guide. You descend the steps silently — one at a time with the fireless torch in hand — until you reach the path and the bench. Before you part, she reminds you to secure your shield and grid around you as you go about your day.

You bow in gratitude to your guide for facilitating the expansive journey of your heart, and for experiencing true unconditional love, bliss and compassion. Receive any remaining messages from her at this time. Know you can meet this guide or others and enter the temple of your heart when you wish. Replace the staff on the left of the bench for your next journey. Now it is time to share your fully activated heart with the external world. Open your eyes, breathe deep, and mirror this inner truth with every step you take. Each step is full of love.

Notes:

Building the Fire

Let us build the fire of transformation and through it experience alchemy.

Note: This ritual is not necessary to enter deeply into the self; it is rather a systematic way to honor the process of letting go and set the stage for inner exploration. Not everything we bring to the fire is negative; to truly surrender into alchemy, we must also offer our most cherished beliefs and truths.

Visualize yourself walking down a path with a bundle of sticks upon your back. Each stick represents an obstacle, challenge, doubt, fear, pain, guilt, shame, goal, hope, dream—all that holds you back and all that propels you forward. You have carried these sticks a long way and you are ready to release their burden of disappointment and expectation. This is the fuel for your fire. You see the fire ring in the distance and you take each step mindfully toward your liberation. Focus your attention on your breath as you take each step closer. Feel the weight of your bundle and contemplate truly surrendering your load.

As you approach the fire ring, you are ready to release everything you believe to be true in order to access the deeper truths within. You set down your bundle and untie the webbing that held it all together. You bow in gratitude for the empty center and honor the ring's power to hold space for transcendence. Now it is time to build your fire, naming each stick that you place into the center, forming a pyramid. Appreciate each upset as a gift while you redirect its energy. Take as much time as you need to complete this process.

When all of what you been holding onto is within this sacred container, take the last piece of wood as an embodiment of yourself, the part you love the most, and offer it to the heavens. As you raise your prize to the sky with your right hand, a flame bursts into form. When you are ready, drop your torch of illumination at the count of three into the frozen beliefs of your old constructs…1…2…3. Let there be freedom, and so it is.

The flames begin to dance through each of your burdens as they release their power of entanglement. The smoke rises and swirls as Spirit clarifies the negative aspects and blockages within you. Listen to the crackles and pops as each stick speaks its truth. Be present with this process and witness the unraveling. Use all of your senses to experience your fire.

The fire blazes with intensity as the heart of liberation begins to open to new possibilities of energy flow. Look through the raging flames into the molten core; this is where alchemy takes place. Alchemy is the process of turning lead to gold, and as the sword masters know, the hottest coals make the strongest steel. Feel the heat and know that complete transformation lies on the inside of this fire. You must be willing to leave behind the familiar and conventional—stepping into the universal laws of trust and faith. When you are ready to leave behind what no longer serves you, take your leap of faith.

Within the fire, you do not burn as a carbon based life form and the heat is not beyond your endurance. Your faith in the process has created a crystalline structure that contributes to your evolution. The fire's offering of purification infiltrates every cell of your body, igniting the dross and transmuting lightness into your being. You begin to dance with the flames and elevate your vision while releasing the last of the debris of your old perception. From this trance state, let yourself completely melt into nothingness to access the fullness of everything that you are. From this state of emptiness where you are beyond form, judgment, preconception, and expectation, OPEN to the journey of self-exploration. Now it is time to go further into your depths. And begin a new journey...

Further contemplation: What will rise from the ashes?

Inner Journeys

Entering the Shadows

It is now time to journey into the depths of who you are. It takes courage to visit your dark corners. As you dive into subterranean realms know that darkness is not a place to fear, rather it's a place to enter with alertness, as your eyes will adjust to see more than your five senses can perceive. The treasure of the mystery resides within the shadows. Light the fire of your heart and may it be your torch along the way. Let us embark on a deeper journey inside.

Imagine yourself in one of your favorite places. Melt into every aspect of this place though your human senses. As you begin to explore your familiar paradise, you notice an opening in the landscape that you have not seen before. Drawn inside, you enter a huge cavern. Light is coming from outside and you can see the expanse of this chamber. The first thing that catches your eye is a series of paintings of red horses running on the surface of the wall—others have been here before. You hear running water and see a small stream flowing into the darkness. The temperature is warmer than you would expect inside this big room and there is a mist in the air. The wet earthy smell nourishes every aspect of being as you ground into this moment.

Light from the external world beams a spotlight onto big formations further into the cave that have been formed over time by dissolved minerals coagulating. You are elated by your discovery and called further into the darkness. As you walk toward the stalactites at the back of the cave, you see a glow within one of the tunnels. Intrigued, you venture into new territory. The surface is uneven so you travel slowly, carefully placing each step. You use your hands, outstretched against the bumpy tunnel walls, to keep your balance. The path continues downward and the light gets brighter. Further down the passageway a torch is waiting for you. When you reach the flame, the tunnel opens into an amphitheater. With the help of the torch you can see your surroundings much more clearly: crystals and formations of various colors and water dripping all around you. You feel the cavern breathing with you, alive and vibrant.

Out of the corner of your eye you see something move. You sense a presence stepping out of the shadows. At first you are startled and fear floods into every pore. Then an old woman in dark robes with a torch in her hand comes toward you. "Do not fear me," she says. "I am the Shadow Queen and I am here to take you further into the earth and more deeply inside yourself. You have shown courage and tenacity to make it this far without a light. Know that the only way to enter the darkness is through its center without doubt or fear. Let faith be your guide. Now let's go!"

Having uttered her abrupt command, the Shadow Queen quickly descends further from the familiar. Carrying your torch in one hand, you run to keep up with her. "We have much to experience within the depths of obscurity. Here we have no point of reference, only the belief in something much bigger than ourselves. It's like the blind leading the blind, literally." The Shadow Queen stops and turns to face you. Her opaline blue eyes speak from experience and you realize she does not see the same spectrum of light that you do. She turns back and continues confidently down the path, leading you through many twists and turns. She comes to a halt outside of a small chamber, lights a torch on the wall, and beckons you inside. As you enter, you are awestruck by what you see. The entire cavern is treasure from floor to ceiling. Gold coins, statues, jewels, and the most intricate tapestries and rugs overflow in piles upon piles. You ask the Shadow Queen to tell you more about this place. She explains, "Lakshmi, the deity of prosperity, reigns here. This is your inner wealth. You forget you have such treasure while on the surface suffering from lack of all sorts. Do not yearn for what you do not have. The external powers that control you by the 'fear and lack' mentality disconnect you from your creative well-spring and inner riches. In reality, you have access to in-finite prosperity within yourself. All you have to do is claim it and bring it to the surface."

Enter the chamber and commune with your treasure. How does it feel to have the support of abundance sur-rounding you? When you are ready, pick one piece from your inner chest to bring back with you. Feel its presence within your pocket. Your adventure continues.

The Shadow Queen leads you further into the cave sys-tem. After many steps, she halts again outside a smaller chamber. Again she lights the torch on the wall and guides you inside. You see mirrors of every shape and size filling the entire surface of the room. "In order to continue on this journey," she explains, "you must be willing and able to completely look at yourself with compassion and forgiveness. There are places within where you have resisted healing and pain resides. It is time to face your demons. Look into your eyes to find the truth. I will be outside if you need me."

Left alone inside the wall of mirrors, you look into every angle of your life. Each mirror reflects a judgment that you have held about yourself, cataloguing all the mistakes, trespasses, disappointments, wrongdoings, and every detour from the path of integrity and truth. The small room gets even smaller as the condescending noise gets louder. At first you feel the weight and pressure of the shadows within, but then you remember what the Shadow Queen imparted and you fearlessly begin to look into the eyes of each image. The rage and the suffering dissipate into an unseen force that strengthens your resolve to continue to dismantle your internal inquisition. You look into your eyes and see only love; it sets you free. The reflections quiet down and you become one with the stillness. You release the shackles of self-judgment and let go of everything that has kept you enslaved. From the fragmented distortions of character, you feel the integrated unity of your full presence.

"Congratulations! You have gone through your greatest obstacle: You!" The Shadow Queen proclaims. "We have one more place to visit on this journey down under. Here you must make total peace with the darkness. Embracing the void can be unsettling—but from emptiness, you will find the well of surrender and open to the divine flow. When you let go of the grip of your expectations, projections and attachments to the outcome, you embody the mystery of divine creation." The Shadow

Queen leads you down a small corridor into an even smaller room with only a cushion. As she beckons you inside she reminds you that you are never alone and that you can always call on your team and inner guidance to assist you. Before she parts she explains, "There is much more to be discovered within the shadows of yourself. Take time to visit these inner caverns and lean into the discomfort. I will be waiting. There is power and strength here that will add dimension to your creative genius and propel purpose into each of your steps."

She leaves no torch and before you can protest she is gone. You are enveloped completely in darkness. As there is nowhere to go and nothing to be, you release into the unraveling of your sense of self. Your definition of who you are melts into nothingness as you become one with the darkness. Rather than a state of despair or defeat you feel a sense of pure potential. Letting go completely opens you up to a presence beyond your perception, to the center of the cosmos where the divine resides. You feel as if you are within the womb of the divine mother, perfectly complete, protected, nurtured and sustained. Transcending your personal agenda has led you to a place of peace and belonging. This is the home deep within you where you are one with all that is. You are a valued piece of the interconnected whole where there is no separation. You realize this is your true essence.

As you humbly accept the gifts of the darkness, you notice the Shadow Queen is gone and you are by yourself in the depths of the earth. You call on your team to assist your return. Some of them you can see, some you can hear, and others you can feel. Your inner sanctum fills with their support and you realize you are never truly alone even in your darkest hour. With this you relax into their benevolent, creative, unconditional embrace, and begin to feel movement through the darkness. You hear the sound of water as your team forms a protective grid around you. You are in an underground river, flowing with the divine. You do not know where you will end up, nor how long it will take, only that you trust the process. And then there is light in the distance.

As you make your transition through the birth canal, you give gratitude for the Shadow Queen guiding you through the abyss within. Her insightful eyes have exposed treasures beyond your wildest imagination. You are inspired by her effortless grace and humble knowing within the shadows. You are no longer afraid of what lurks in the dark as you have reclaimed your prosperity, your worthiness, your integrated wholeness with all that is, and have felt the loving support of your team though it all. Now it is time to re-enter the world.

Turning the Dial Up

After you jump into the fire of alchemy, [2] you find your-self in the middle of a command center. From your van-tage point, you see levers, dials, buttons of all shapes and sizes, lights blinking on and off, and in the corner of your vision—a big red button with red letters screaming DO NOT PUSH>SYSTEM RESET. Recording equipment, tape reels, and projectors line one wall of the room while sounds and images of your lifetime memories fill many screens throughout. Two round windows bring light in-to this space and flank a translucent orb that shimmers between them. A gigantic chair in front of the center con-sole urges you to reclaim the throne within your own mind. This is your motherboard, and we are here today to fine tune how you experience reality.

From outside your immediate sight you hear, "Turn it up!" You look around to see where the voice is coming from. "I am outside of your head. Look out one of your eyes and you will be able to see me." You dart to the round window, and sure enough, you are looking into a

---

[2] Refer to Building the Fire meditation on page 59

familiar landscape: your everyday world—a guy in a chair with a megaphone and a fancy hat appears to be floating in the air. "Hello! Hiya is my name. I'm the director of your 'life story'; let's make some internal adjustments so you can transcend the mundane." He shouts, "What are you waiting for?" Before you heed his adamant command, you question Hiya's presence. You ask how long he has been with you and if he is there for your greatest good. He explains that he is part of your internal guidance system and has been with you since the beginning as part of the team for your greatest good. He adds that he stays out of your field of vision to record the most authentic footage of your life experience. You ask his intention and he confirms his genuine interest in the advancement of your soul's learning.

"Sometimes you forget why you are here. I am here to remind you what you are capable of and set up reinforcements within your command center. Before we begin, ask anything that is not of the highest vibration of benevolent, creative, unconditional love to leave now. Good. Now see that system override switch? Flip it up and put the "fog" flash drive into its slot. Good! Now you are completely offline, with added interference to impede any attempts of remote manipulation. Go ahead and initiate the antivirus to debug any parasites that have been sucking off your energy fields. Good! There are forces and ancient agendas designed to keep you in a subservient role. Lack, despair, and fear have rendered you separate, powerless, controllable. It is time for you to be the sovereign being that you are and access the expansion of your destiny. Go ahead and retune your channel to freedom and divine purpose." You tune into the 528 Hz signal, the love frequency. Before moving to the next panel of your motherboard Hiya adds, "This station facilitates your DNA repair and healing on all levels. Ahhh… so much better!

"First, let's do an overall system boost so you can perform to your highest potential. Push the defragment button; anything that is sluggish or unnecessary for your personal growth will be condensed, filtered through your greatest good, and stored for a later time. This integration allows for a smoother and more effective operation for your tasks at hand." After "defragging" you begin to feel less scattered, more present and aware of yourself. Hiya points out many gauges all grouped together under the automatic function control panel, including heartbeat, blood flow, oxygen intake, metabolism, waste removal, reproduction, and hormone balance. Hiya explains, "If there are breakdowns in any of these systems in the future, this is where to begin your healing process. There are specialists who can read your internal data and restore optimal perfor-

mance. When the time is right, they will present themselves." You record a note to self and continue the tour
within your internal mechanism.

"OK, are you ready to 'turn it up'?" Hiya directs you to
a blue dial with numbers on it. "Go ahead and turn that
dial from 7 to 9. This will affect the range and capacity
of your vibrational frequency. The nine setting will open
channels for greater clairvoyance, lucid dreaming, syn-
chronistic encounters, and the ability to quantum jump
within your reality; more on that later. This adjustment
stimulates the pineal gland and awakens the third eye.
Go ahead and look through your central channel." You
effortlessly turn the blue dial to nine then make your
way to the opalescent globe. You peer through the lens
and witness a world of energy moving with vibrant colors and geometric shapes that you never knew existed.
Similarly to gazing through a kaleidoscope of your
childhood, you are in awe as you observe the fabric of
reality with your inner eye.

"You can access this clarity of vision when you have
stillness within," Hiya explains. "There is much to learn
about sacred geometry and your place within it; all in
good time. While you are there, go ahead and adjust
your eyesight to 20/20." Reluctantly you leave the
interweaving patterns of your inner sight and resume

your system upgrade. You turn the rings to 20 on the inside of each socket. Your vision is crisp and precise when you look through the portals. "Congratulations! Now you no longer need external lenses to view the 3D world!" Hiya cheers.

"There is a dial next to your ear ports. Turn it up to the next octave. With this adjustment you will be able to hear the higher realms and receive messages more clearly with your clairaudience." As instructed you modify the range of sound near your inner ear vestibule. You begin to hear a ringing in your ears and tones enter your new sense of hearing. "Good. Listen and pay attention when there are changes in your auditory input. This fluctuation of pitch most likely indicates a form of communication being transmitted—ask your team to help decipher any foreign idioms unfamiliar to your knowledge. Also, begin to hone your skill of telepathy. Much like developing a muscle, practice the art of sending and receiving messages to become more proficient at it. In the not so distant future, a lot of communication will be beyond the spoken word.

"The last meter we will look at today, even though there are many more, is the brainwave detector that measures your thoughts." You look at your meter; it is pulsing back and forth in a sporadic rhythm. Hiya continues,

"When you find stillness within the chaos of your mind, you are able to receive insights and feel a state of well-being. The zero point is the best place to make decisions and ask for guidance. It is easy to get distracted in the endless stream of data filling your perception; now you have a meter to help you think clearly. When you create stillness within, the external world begins to reflect this state of mind." You sit in the middle of Hiya's tour and concentrate on the present moment, breathing evenly in and out. You watch the meter calm its movement and rest at zero. An inner peace permeates your entire being.

Before you drift into bliss, your attention is called back to the screens surrounding you. Each screen is playing a different memory loop. Hiya welcomes you back and explains, "These memories have made the most impact in your 'life story'. You have the opportunity to replay some scenes that have created heaviness in your heart. This is the time to say the unsaid and release the burdens of guilt and shame. Before we take a walk down memory lane, know that there are no mistakes. Everything happens for a reason even if it is not understood at the time. There is perfect order within the chaos."

Hiya cues up one of the most profound moments in your life, and when you are ready he calls, "Action!"

The projected image on the screen is a life-sized holo-gram of the person, place or thing you are ready to con-front. Take as much time as you need to speak the unsaid. When the process is complete, the hologram disappears and the screen is empty. Repeat this cycle to clear out any unfinished business and defuse any emo-tional release you may experience—no more than five screens at a time. "Cut, it's a wrap!" Hiya calls.

Next, you are instructed to dismantle the negative self-talk that has played in the backdrop of your mind. The reels of your old belief structures and unhealthy pat-terns are heavy and worn. You disengage the auto-play settings and remove their burden. Feeling lighter, Hiya directs you to a box that says "hope and inspiration" on top of it. You open the box—inside are modern movie reels. You feed the films into the projectors and new im-ages appear upon a few of your screens. You see smiling faces, kids laughing, lovers holding hands, people work-ing together in a community garden, youth planting trees, a group picking up trash, circles of men and women gathering together to share visions and truth, people caring for each other, lots of love, affirmations, inspiring quotes, art, dance, music, all forms of creative expression. Your heart sings with every image. "These images are here to remind you to stay positive when you begin to feel despair within the current world drama," Hiya explains. "Remember, life is but a dream. It is an illusion, a projection of light; you can change it and slice through it with your focused attention."

"Your 'life story' has become a manual for new initiates. You have shown courage and dedication with the process. Even through the moments of despair when you lost faith, you always came back to hope, trust, and belief in the bigger picture and the higher power. I commend you and your resilience; need I say it is only the beginning. Buckle up, young Jedi warrior, you have a lot more of life to live and a multitude of experiences to share on your journey of self-mastery. Life has a way of turning up the dial when you do. With your override status, enhanced senses and refined settings, you will experience life in a whole new way. We are all here with you as your witness. Please know that YOU are the change you wish to see in the world."

You thank Hiya for his guidance and support during your system upgrade. When you peer through your central sight you realize Hiya looks familiar. He has your imprint and it dawns on you that you have been working with your higher self this whole time. You feel honored to have made this connection to your internal wisdom and dedicate each moment to being fully tuned in and turned on. With this quantum leap, you are operating at your highest capacity, fully activated within the present moment. You continue to put one foot in front of the next as the world spins around you. You are the eye of the storm.

Notes:

Transcending the Human Experience:

A New Sense of Self

This journey leads you beyond the 3rd dimension physical form to explore dimensions of energy through your upper chakra system. There are many tools, capabilities and knowledge unique to you to be accessed through these centers outside of the "perceived" human experience. You will venture from the tactile and dense version of reality into the essence of vibration and frequency. Once the information is received, integrated and assimilated into your human experience, you become an inspiration for humanity.

You will enter this journey through the temple of the heart. [3] After you have activated your heart, fully expanding it infinitely in all directions, experienced true compassion, and collected its essence back into your heart space, you are ready to begin.

---

[3] Refer to Heart Temple Activation meditation on page 53

Inside your heart temple you notice a glowing spiral staircase of golden light in a remote corner that you may not have noticed before. At the bottom stair is a sign on the chain blocking off entry that reads, "All who enter here must know compassion." You have touched unconditional love in its purest form and have become formless within it. You know compassion and are confident in unclipping the sign to allow your passage further up the stairway to the heavens. As you begin your journey upward, you hear ringing in your ears and feel electricity in each step.

Around the next bend there is a landing with a coat stand and a second sign that reads, "Hang your human space suit here ..." As you puzzle over this instruction, a golden orb descends to meet you. Inside your head you hear, "My name is Evatar from the Great Central Sun and I am here to assist you today on your journey into the multidimensional realms within yourself. I am part of the team for your greater good. You will not need your human form for this journey. There is a zipper behind your right ear that has always been there and it follows the right side of your body. When you are ready, go ahead and unzip your human space suit, release your light body from this prior identity and hang it here." You do as instructed without judgment and experience a sensation of liberation from density. Feel your new sense of self.

As you witness yourself, you are still in the shape of a human form, and yet you are pure light and energy. You glide up the stairway effortlessly. Evatar pauses to explain: "You are now entering the realms of the divine within your energy body. This is where we access your connection to Source, develop your psychic centers and abilities, activate your dormant DNA, and transcend duality—the structure of reality. We will stop at each center of higher knowledge, pay homage to the essence that permeates each realm, and uncover what you are meant to receive along the way."

You struggle to understand these words, yet you know you must trust the journey further into the unknown. You continue up the spiral staircase to the next landing. Evatar turns and says, "This is the energy center of divine love, spiritual compassion, karmic residue, and the activation of spiritual skills. As you sit in the center of the lotus, take a bird's eye view of your human existence and notice any patterns of relationships and behaviors. When you see twists in the energy flow, use your keys of evolution to unlock yourself from the karmic bonds." With these words Evatar evaporates into the eighth chakra.

You sit inside the lotus and see yourself inside your story, in the middle of a web that passes through and around you. You notice where there are breaks in some of the energy lines and loops in others. You investigate the disruption of flow, listen to its discord, and see how it has played out in your life. Some of the patterns were created by misunderstandings or misguided truths passed on from your family lineage and past life experiences, others have been programmed through social conditioning. As you are an expert artist of the finest tapestries, you infuse forgiveness and unconditional love through each strand and line of connection, resolving all shame, guilt, pain and suffering. You weave completion into your web of evolution. As you witness your energy flow to be clean and clear, you free yourself from karmic residue and are able to access the full spectrum of divine love. Feel this freedom.

Evatar reappears. "Very nice," she says. "This is so beautiful. You are connected with everyone and everything, and feel the love of the divine. Your soul family has agreed to help you in this life by sometimes playing the villain. The earth is the school for your soul's refining." With that she leads you back to the staircase and continues to spiral up. On the next landing she explains, "This is the energy center of your soul's blueprint. This is where you can access all the skills and abilities learned in all lifetimes. Similar to the Akashic records that record all lifetimes of all souls, your blueprint is a unique set of codes stored in your DNA. When you translate your data you are able to uncover your gift and the mission you are here to bring forth in the present time." And then she again disappears, this time into the ninth chakra.

As you sit inside the lotus once again, you place your energetic hands on two glowing orbs on either side of you. The orbs read your essence and a screen appears revealing many numbers, shapes and colors that portray your unique composition. You begin to see layers upon layers of similar codes under each blueprint. You sense these were the previous expressions of your soul embodied. Each blueprint is unique, but they all have a similar pattern. The top blueprint is the summation of all the roles you played and mastered through the ages. A band of light passes over your eye center and finally you are able to crack the code and understand the language of your soul. As you look through yourself, you now see both the physical manifestation and the energetic essence of each blueprint; you are aware of both the struggles of defeat and the gifts of service. Take as much time as you need to tap into lives and to access the knowledge and wisdom you are here to remember.

Evatar reappears when your exploration is complete. "Do you see that you have been many different aspects of yourself and mastered everything you need to know already? All you have to do is tap into your soul's blueprint to access what you have forgotten. You are the wealth of all of your experiences, and this is your gift to bring to humanity at this time. All of your lives have prepared you for this moment. When you know your service, you become fully activated within the human matrix. You can come back here any time to access more information embedded deep within your cells." With that she is off once again, into the higher realms of knowledge.

As you venture further up the helix, you come to another landing, catching up to Evatar once again. She explains, "This is the energy center where you are able to transcend duality and unify the polarities within yourself. The divine union of the masculine and feminine must occur, enabling your divine creativity. You cannot have one pole without the other. Becoming the Tao and merging the yin and the yang, you will also begin to notice the synchronicities of dynamic energies at play to assist you in bringing forth your gifts through your experience." With that, she is gone. As you sit within the lotus of the tenth chakra, you feel a stirring inside as you begin to unify polar expressions of the feminine and masculine. While you embrace the receptive, magnetic, negative charges of yin and the active, electric, positive charges of yang, you feel the mixing of elements generating energy. Cultivating this charge restores balance in your core. Going beyond the internal movement, you find a fully charged stillness resting within. You realize that through the pulse of opposites resides integration into wholeness.

Evatar drifts back into your center and says, "You are a co-creator of your reality. From the state of stillness plant a seed of intention and divine flow will provide the synchronicity for fruition of your vision. The final outcome may not appear the way you envisioned it, but know that the forces at work are conspiring for your greatest good. Honor all parts of yourself and the experience duality has shown you to see your intricate qualities. You are no longer operating through separation and control; you are coming into alignment with creation and the divine oneness." Again she drifts further up the stairway into the brightness of high vibration; you follow humbly behind.

Evatar stops on the next landing and leads you to the eleventh energy center. "This is the place where you are able to access the advanced spiritual skills of travel beyond the limits of time and space: teleporting, multilocation, parallel realities, and instant manifestation, to name a few. As you know, the structure of life is much more than you have been taught. Today you will get a taste of what you are capable of—yet these skills take some practice to hone. Be patient." As you have become accustomed to her sudden disappearances, you are not surprised to find her gone.

You are very curious about what will happen as you sit within the lotus of the eleventh chakra. Instantaneously you are transported to a clear room with five openings. As you inspect the openings, they turn into tunnels that are also clear, each with a bright golden spiral coursing into the abyss. Every aperture looks the same yet they all lead into different directions. As you decide which path to take, you remember what Evatar said about the quantum world and the ability to bend reality. You decide to explore all of the spirals at the same time. You are not sure how you are doing it, but you can literally move in five directions at once. You continue through all the tunnels simultaneously until they open up into another world.

From one vantage point, you see a world of vibrant color that seems to be floating in the atmosphere. You see blue people flying in little crafts. You want to explore more, but today you decide to stay on the edge of this world and watch. From another vantage point, you experience blinding golden light. A harmony of chimes play in high frequencies and you notice hints of wings in the distance. Again, you would like to explore further, but you decide to sit on the edge of the tunnel and observe. From yet another vantage point, you witness the familiar hustle and bustle of traffic on a busy street corner. You see a flower shop and happy faces leaving with bundles of flowers to deliver to their loved ones. An older man stops and gives a woman, battered from years on the streets, a beautiful red rose. You hear him say, "I honor you today," as he looks into her eyes and bows. From another vantage point you see only darkness with a hint of light in the distance. You listen and you hear the drip of water in the far reaches of the chasm. You know there is much to experience in the depths of the void, but again it is an experience for another day. From another vantage point you see lines of energy shifting into variable patterns and color waves. There is a buzzing sound as the lines crisscross in motion to an unseen rhythm. You are curious where this world leads, but again today you are here only to witness. Now you bring your attention back to your energy body standing in the center of the clear room, yet you are still able to expand awareness to all concurrent viewpoints. One step further and you are back sitting in the center of the lotus. Feel your full awareness of all possibilities.

After a pause, Evatar returns to join you. "Very well done! As you can see this is only the beginning. There is much more to experience through each of these portals, which are endless, by the way. Did I mention super powers? Now you know that time and space are limited human constructs. They are superimposed on infinite possibilities to keep order and definition. You are a multidimensional being able to experience the quantum in all capacities. Imagine the possibilities of your human potential. We have one more stop on our journey today." And she makes her final ascent up the stairway.

As you reach the top of the landing within the twelfth energy center, you see golden light swirling in all directions. You also see a faint set of stairs leading further upward, and you ask Evatar about this place. "This is the home of the divine, where we come when we are ready to ascend into the 5th dimension of existence and beyond. This is also a landing zone to access your connection to the cosmos as well as beings from the places beyond perception. There is so much more for your soul to experience when the time is right. Who knows? Maybe someday you will join us at the round table and help us better understand the human condition so we can protect and assist this plane of free will. One day we will all meet again in the Great Central Sun where I am currently residing. Until then, know your mission is important. Do not get lost in the delusion of external fulfillment—this is one lesson your soul is ready to complete that will release you from the 3D loop. Also, do not get lost in exploring the upper realms of existence. Anchor all you have learned here today into your human form. We know there are many challenges on the journey of your human timeline yet know we are all with you. Keep faith in love and serve your gifts to humanity.

"Oh, and by the way, don't forget to zip back into your human space suit before you return." With that she is gone. As you sit in the center of the lotus within the twelfth chakra, you experience pure bliss and communion with the divine. Feel this infusion. You are one with the divine; it is not outside of yourself. You feel complete, at peace, inspired. You also feel your interconnectedness with all beings and can see the divine within every soul. You realize everyone is a piece of you as you are a piece of them; all a reflection of the divine. You vow to honor everyone's soul spark even when they do not recognize it themselves. You bow to Evatar's omnipresence on this journey of higher wisdom. You know there is so much more to experience within all upper energy centers, but now it is time to return to the present. You drift back down the double helix to where your human form awaits. You realize that all twelve of your DNA strands (steps) are ignited to their full capacity where some were dormant before. You have tasted your human potential and have facilitated a pathway to your soul's higher wisdom. As you step into your identity, you know that fully charged, you are much more than meets the eye. As you return to the comfort of your heart temple, you are fully activated and ready to share your gifts with the world, with a new lightness in your step.

Contemplative Journeys

Shapeshifting Form

You will begin this journey today through the alchemy of the fire. [4] From the center of the fire, you are able to drop your form into the formless. As you let go of your identity, you open yourself up to the world of possibilities. There is a lot to learn from the creatures upon the earth.

Within the void, you become aware of your body shifting into a new form. You begin to see through five windowed lenses and perceive the energetic realms. Your body is light as your iridescent wings lift you up. You are following the productivity pulse innate within your nature that commands you to complete a mission for your Queen. Your acute senses draw you to a field of lotuses. As you land in the middle of a lotus, your six feet begin to dance upon the surface, collecting pollen into the sacs at your sides. You sip the nectar from the center of the flower and store it in your stomach for later. When you complete the harvest of one flower, you continue through the field of lotuses until you are fully

---

[4] Refer to Building the Fire meditation on page 59

loaded with the fruits of your labor. Before you return, you stop by some tree blossoms along the way to collect sap to fix the damage the hive received in the last storm.

The pheromones from the Queen lead you back to the hive. Upon your arrival you begin to dance your lotus dance to send others to your new found reserve. As you enter the hustle of workers coming and going, you deliver your pollen to the nursery, where it will be used as food for the babies. You know you will not be able to see the Queen, as she is deep within her chambers at the center of the hive. You regurgitate the nectar from your body into a honeycomb cell that another worker has just repaired at the far end of the hive. Yet another worker uses her wings to fan the liquid to dry the excess moisture. This sweet liquid is what will sustain the hive throughout the cold winter months. You deliver the propolis to the workers in charge of weatherproofing the hive; the sticky sap is instantly used to quell a draft from the outside. You are then prepared to take another flight for the hive, as there is much work to be done, knowing that the sweetness of your life is the byproduct. You follow the directions to the next dance of devotion. Feel your Bee essence.

Again there is a void as you become aware of your body shifting into a new form. You sense yourself high above the ground in a tree big enough to support your strong muscular body. You see nocturnal movement come to life with calm focus. Through the moonlit shadows, your keen eyesight takes in every detail as you decide which prey will feed your appetite tonight. You see a monkey swinging through the trees, but a gazelle drinking from a nearby watering hole catches your attention. With anticipation in each step, you slowly pick your way down the tree in stealth mode, navigating branches along the way. As you crouch down and crawl through the reeds along the edge of the oasis to get a better look, you see more than one gazelle drinking her fill. They sense your presence and stop mid-sip to scope the scene. Now is your chance. You blast out of your hiding place in full gait and spook your catch. With intentional movement, chasing their wild surprise, you outrun the smaller of the two beasts. You bite into her skull and the game is over. You drag your kill back up the tree, enjoy the rewards of your agility, and continue to thrive. Feel your Jaguar essence.

Again there is a void, and you become aware of your body shifting into a new form. You are in darkness. Cooler temperatures have signaled you to burrow deep within the earth and hibernate. Time passes, seasons change, and now you are ready to leave your subterranean nest, feed yourself, and lie in the heat of the sun.

You sense the vibration of movement above your comfortable niche, which stimulates your motivation to resurface. As your scales grip the path upward, you feel your skin molting off. Without resistance, you release your old expression. You find your new rhythm through this transformation as you glide your body from side to side, allowing your kundalini to rise. You welcome the warmth and brightness of the external world and reawaken your vital energy. You are attracted to a rock and lie upon it to warm your blood and witness the flow of healing within your body. After a time, you are ready to hunt. With your keen sense of smell through the tongue that flickers in and out of your mouth, you discover a little mouse den nearby. You slither your way into the hole and it is not long before you find your prize. Returning to your lair to digest your prey, you make yourself comfortable. For the next few weeks you will lay low, integrating renewed life into your cells. Feel your Snake essence.

Again there is a void as you become aware of your body shifting into a new form. You feel weightless as your enormous body drifts effortlessly through the blue-green landscape surrounding you. There are plentiful kelp beds that sway with the tide and expand as far as your eye can see. Much to your delight, schools of krill are close by and you dive in to get your fill. Then with the speed of your dolphin cousins, you launch yourself through the glassy surface; life-sustaining oxygen enters your lungs. In one instant you are flying with the warmth of sunlight hitting your skin; in the next density causes a huge spray of seawater in your wake. You hear your pod's song of ancient history echoing in the distance. Heeding the call, you swim toward the harmonic resonance and feel the urge to flourish within the universal mind. As you have recorded time from the beginning, the cycle continues, and now it is time to migrate south for the cooler months ahead. Your pod begins the heart song to gather and line up with the electromagnetic compass. You join the song, bellowing your soul's truth while weaving your body through various fins and tails—a flow of collective movement. Feel your Whale essence.

Again there is a void and you become aware of your body shifting into a new form. You climb high into the branches of your new home. You release your expectation on the wind as you let the first line drift from you. It catches the other side of hope; you attach the thread and anchor the bridge from the dream to the manifest. Your delicate long legs balance on the finest silk of your making. You anchor the frame threads that span the distance in between and connect the center to the radius. Once all the points have been set, you weave your fate. You spin a spiral of sticky film, careful not to become entangled in your web of illusion. After your trap is complete, you inspect your craftsmanship and monitor the vibration of the entire structure with all eight legs and all eight eyes. If there is any sensation detected, you will feel it through the signal line. Adding pheromones that lure the unsuspecting traveler, you retreat from your creation into the dark shadows and wait. Your hiatus is cut short when you feel your first sign of struggle. You respond quickly, effortlessly maneuvering along your intricate design, injecting venom into your catch, and wrapping it in silk threads while it turns to liquid for easy digestion. Destiny has fed your mystery. Feel your Spider essence.

Again there is a void and you become aware of your body shifting into a new form. With regal authority you look out to the horizon; your intent eyes witness every detail and movement. You are nestled in an aerie that you had made with your mate, composed of sticks, twigs, and soft grasses from the forest floor. Now, you are incubating future life, patiently waiting for your fledglings to break out of their shells when the time is right; protecting them with the warmth of your feathers from the inevitable storm coming. You see your mate coasting in the distance, returning with victory in his talons. Once you share his catch and change duties, you step to the edge of your sanctuary, spread your eight-foot wingspan, and let freedom take you high into the sky. As you soar above the mundane, you feel the breath of Spirit moving through you. The force of the tempest approaching plays through every filament of your being and you find your way through her grip to where the salmon are swimming upstream to spawn. Without pause you swoop down, swiftly pierce through the pink flesh, and catch the drift back to your nest. Your majesty returns, before the skies disperse, to the delicate eggs of life and prepares for the storm. Feel your Eagle essence.

Through this journey of form we have learned that our animal instincts are without emotion and our actions are based on survival. Whether it is the hive mind or a loner predatory approach, the focus is the same: Become one with the environment, have patience for the right timing, harvest only what is needed, and the circle of life continues. As we are interconnected with all that is, the animal kingdom has much to teach us. May we humbly experience the raw essence of survival of the fittest. This insight may facilitate understanding of what it takes to co-exist within the wild portions of ourselves. To adventure through form and integrate through each essence outside of our species adds depth to our compassion for all of creation. May we begin to look at existence with a new set of eyes.

A Journey through the Elements

This journey will lead you into the five elements of the human experience. Water. Air. Earth. Fire. Spirit. We cannot have one element without the other, as they work together to create life as we know it. Breathe deep, center yourself, and enjoy the ride.

From the stillness within, your senses become immersed in the liquid that sustains you and makes up most of your human form. You are the sanctuary for life within the ocean tides, drifting with the ebb and the flow. You are the river currents cutting deep ravines with the precision of time. Condensing into critical mass, you fall from great heights to nourish tender garden greens. You are the swirling tempest at sea becoming a typhoon both destructive and restorative as you slice through everything within your path. Collected from a well in a small plastic bucket and carried miles to your destination, you are consumed by all living things. You are the flash flood unleashing your power through layers of history removing all obstacles within your wake. You are Water; a synergistic structure of hydrogen and oxygen atoms.

From the depths of your element, Yemaya, the guardian of water, rises to speak on your behalf.

"Listen dearest children of the earth, hear my heartfelt plea. I reside within the depths of the oceans, coexisting with the debris and byproducts of modern man, where there is much sickness. I ask for you all to become aware of the daily assaults to our lifeline and take the future into your own hands. Learn to conserve and protect this precious resource that sustains life on this planet; the alternative is dismal. The time is NOW! Use your powerful minds to clear the negative karma placed within our waterways as big businesses capitalize and hoard our essential elixir of life. Use your positive vibrations to enhance the geometric arrangement of your drinking water's molecules; this crystalline form can facilitate detoxification on all levels. We need your help to co-create change and restore balance. Visualize water running freely from its source to the mighty oceans, clean and clear, while nourishing all life in its path. May you never thirst! This is my wish, this is my vision."

With that Yemaya looks through your eyes and peers into your heart. You bow in deep gratitude for her words of truth and her call to action. As you have become one with the element of water, depending upon its gift to sustain the very nature of your existence, you feel the weight of Yemaya's plea. You align with the Council of Water and vow to serve and protect this resource as fellow guardian. Take a moment to integrate into the league and decide what you can do today to heed the call.

From the stillness within, you merge with the light breeze that drifts upon the earth's surface cooling the overheating core. As your force picks up strength, you lift sand and dirt in circular twists giving life to the sedentary. You are a blast of current that generates more energy to add to the forces of change. Unable to harness, your gusts exceed expected measurements, creating funnels of transformation. You rip apart the damaged, cut through the solid, shake up the inflexible, push the boundaries of limitation, and join forces with the other elements to transform all structure. You are the calm after the storm, the upheaval settled. You are the element of Air: a mixture of oxygen, nitrogen, argon, helium, methane, carbon dioxide and other gases and microbes. The oxygen within you sustains most life upon the planet. The plant kingdom renews your element with an exchange of molecules, creating more clean air to breathe. From the spaces in between Oya, Orisha of the winds, guardian of the air makes her presence known.

"I am Oya. I come here today to speak to the children of Earth and ask you to look inside yourselves to find where the tempest resides. This is the place where we can access the call to action. The air we breathe is in danger of toxic overload. Not only have industrialization and modern advances wreaked havoc on our inhalation, covert agendas assault us daily with 'chemtrails' and 'bio-engineered' weather modification known as HAARP (High Frequency Active Auroral Research Program). The pollution raining down on our food and water supplies is poisoning our cellular structure. We can no longer look away from the thinning of our atmosphere and the holes within our ozone that allow harmful rays to enter. As solar flares continue to bombard our planet and our magnetosphere weakens, superstorms rage across the surface of man. It is time to think how your carbon footprint affects the air we intake. Drive your car less, ride your bike, walk, use public transportation, carpool more. Be mindful of products consumed and power sources tapped into; support alternative solutions—wind turbines, solar panel technology, and carbonless vehicles. Educate yourselves, rally with elected officials who support the Clean Air Act, and demand changes of policy. It is time to speak up and let the wind carry your words."

With this, Oya rises and fills the entire sky. Her stormy eyes pierce into your commitment. You bow in deep gratitude for her words of truth and her call to action. As you have become one with the element of air, depending upon its gift to sustain your very existence, you feel the weight of Oya's command. You align with the Council of Air and vow to serve and protect this element as fellow guardian. Take a moment to integrate into the league and decide what you can do today to heed the call.

From the stillness you smell the rich soil of your making. Within your folds reside shelters made of your flesh where all of creation takes sanctuary to hibernate, restore balance, and harmonize with your tune. You feel circles of feet dancing to the rhythm of your heartbeat, singing ancient songs of wisdom. You are the highest mountain peak and the deepest canyon. You are the sandy beach and the densest jungle. You feel the burning sensation as chemicals are injected into your muscles to release your liquid gold. You feel big machines ripping precious gems from your insides, pillaging all and giving nothing back. You feel explosions of ignorance rage war upon your back, rocking you to the core. You shift and shake old paradigms of control while your molten blood recreates tomorrow. You feel the interplay with the other elements through your pores, feeding your hearty roots. You become one with Earth, feel her pain and celebrate her fierce power and grace. From the depths of your foundation, Gaia rises to the surface.

"I am Gaia, Earth Mother. I speak to the children of the earth, listen to my call. I ask you to put down your gadgets of technology and lie naked upon my chest. Come to me and remember why you are here. Slow down your pace and commune within my arms to hear my song and fill your depleted wells. There is much treachery taking place among mortal men to capitalize on my gifts, creating separation and discord among the human family. My dearest children, many of you have lost sight that everything comes from me and will one day return. I give myself freely to you so you may never hunger. Put your hands in the dirt, plant seeds in the fertile soil, nourish your roots, and watch them grow. Enjoy the bounty of the harvest from within my belly for I am the mother of all things. This will sustain you and the future generations. Do not fear when I resettle myself and cause upheaval. Know that everything has its rightful place within the window of time. I am your advocate to thrive upon your home within the cosmic dance. I ask that you co-create with me as I continue to support your efforts to unite and inspire the whole. Help protect me and all living kingdoms suckling upon my breasts through sustainable action. I honor you today for your contribution and conscious awareness of your impact within the grid. Know that I love you unconditionally."

Gaia looks deeply into your eyes with her kind yet wild expression and speaks to your heartbeat, an echo of her own. She has seen many years come and go and will continue to exist with or without the human family upon her. The earth element ignites the passion within you to nurture and protect your home. You are reminded to take action daily to counterbalance the lack of awareness and teach alternative ways of existence by example. You honor the gifts you receive every day from Gaia and you choose to be a part of the Earth Council and become a caretaker. Take a moment to integrate into the league of Earth Keepers.

From the stillness within, you feel heat rise from your belly. A flash fills the air with brilliant light and a clash of electrostatic discharge. You are created. At first you are a spark of light on the earth igniting into a small flame, slowly building your strength of character. Your flames dance upon the external, consuming decomposed life. With the addition of the wind feeding your element, your temperament rages, fueling transformation within your path. The black scar of scorched earth births a new beginning. When your power is harnessed and

111

intentional, you tenderize sustenance for the human family. You are the center of attention as a group of women collect around you, paying homage to your light and sharing their visions into the evening hours. You are an integral part of the cycle of life, you are Fire. From the alchemy of transcendence, Pele appears before you in her full glory.

"I am Pele. I am the guardian of the fire and I am here to speak to the children of the earth. I speak for the force within that propels you to fulfill your dreams and goals. I ask you to hold the charge of your vision. Do not give up faith and let your will falter. Rather than blazing trail and burning everything within your path, temper your torch and walk with an activated focus balanced in grace. You are powerful beyond measure; the heat of your passion can dissolve limited belief systems very quickly. To avoid burnout, remember to feed your vision and sustain your endurance with quiet determination. Now is a time of great change and we need your full participation. You are a part of the revolution. Instead of burning down the system, let us infiltrate and dismantle the structures man has devised to the detriment of the natural world; our aim is to bring the elements back to their rightful place at center stage. I feel your pain and suffering as you witness the atrocities happening upon Earth currently; simmer your pulse to create the most effective change. Ground your inner fire and cultivate the shifts you wish to see in this world. Respect the destructive power of the fire, and it will honor you in return. The Council of Fire is complete."

With these words, you feel Pele's heat infuse your core with hope for a new day. She melts into the center of your abdomen and becomes a pillar of strength within your step. You vow to use the power of the fire wisely, with honor and respect. Rather than destroying everything that is corrupt, you choose to become a guardian of the fire, actively participate within the world of man, and represent truth for a sustainable tomorrow, a realization of your vision. Take a moment to fully integrate your presence into the Council of Fire.

From the stillness, you feel a stirring deep within your soul. You nurture a crying child with a compassionate touch. You give hope to the tortured man sitting in his prison cell facing his demise. You are the awakening of the corporate CEO to the destructive footprint of his trade, you are curing the insatiable appetite of the consumer for things he does not need. You are the creative spark in the artist painting optimistic visions of tomorrow. You are the passionate love shared between soulmates reunited through time and space. You are present as a youth kneels before plant medicine with deep respect, honoring the open doors within her mind. You are an empathetic hand that reaches through the darkness of internal struggle and shines light toward the horizon of freedom. You are the laughter of children at play, oblivious to how the money wheel perpetuates the bind of living paycheck to paycheck. You are the force that encourages the broken spirit to fight the "good fight" against all odds and keep faith in the victory. You are the breath of Spirit. From the hara point above your navel, Kali appears before you.

"I am Kali, the creator and destroyer of all things, the guardian of Spirit. I come here today to speak to the children of the earth. I ask you to remember the bigger picture of your existence. Not all has been lost. You are here to care for the elements and through your heart, reflect the essence of Spirit, beyond judgment, anger and hate. There is no separation between you and your fellow man nor plant, animal or mineral kingdoms. When you recognize the common thread of divinity, however distorted it may appear, liberation from the shackles of control and domination is yours to claim. United you change the current state of affairs for the greatest good of all. You are the hope and the plea for a new day. As the creator, know that I am within you. As the destroyer, know I am within you as well, for we two are not separate. We are part of the whole, a dynamic dance between polarity and duality. My wish is for all of creation to overcome conflict, pierce through the veils of illusion that oppress your gifts, heal the chasms within your hearts, and create peace upon Earth. The power of choice is within all of you to lay down your weapons and build new foundations to thrive together. The alternative is to experience my wrath and bring mass destruction to all that has been created. You are the choice, you are the future."

Kali's power of creation and destruction humbles you. You drop to your knees and accept the call to action. You choose to see Spirit between the spaces that divide and separate as a daily practice. You select to exist beyond a self-serving paradigm, put your ego in check, and move from an inspired heart-centered place. You become the vehicle to serve the whole of humanity. You are a guardian of Spirit as you walk upon the earth. Take a moment to integrate into the league of service.

You have chosen to uphold your commitment to protect and serve the five sacred elements of life. Your existence becomes an interplay of these elements, and you a force of nature. This walk is not for the faint of heart, and at times it may appear to be a lonely road. Yet, as you align with Yemaya, Oya, Gaia, Pele, and Kali and take your place within the council of each element, you know you are not alone, far from it. You remember why you volunteered to be here at this time and you take your place on the front lines.

A Call to Action for the Seventh Generation

After you have listened to the council of each element, you are asked to journey through your family lineage. By doing this, you are able to better understand who has brought you to the present moment, as well as how your actions might influence the next seven generations. You will find both glory and flaw intertwined into perfection, as your family lineage has played and continues to play its part perfectly within your spectrum of growth. During this meditation observe the common characteristics that course through your bloodline.

Note: This journey is not designed to offend anyone or bring up angst. The family lineage can be a sensitive subject for some. There may be emotional or physical violations present within your ancestral blood line. If necessary, extract yourself from your personal experiences and take a bird's eye view of the collective human past. Whether or not you procreate, you can act in favor of future generations. If you do not have children, travel through the lineage of someone close to you during this meditation.

Anchor yourself into the present moment and prepare to explore what forces within your lineage brought you to this point. Behind you, you see your parents in their full glory. Not only do you see the cracks and crevices that molded your perception of the world, you see the victories and sacrifices they each made to bring you to this moment. From this vantage point, you are able to see your parents' motivations and responses to life more clearly. Where there has been strife in the fabric of the family unit, you now have compassion for the choices they made with what they had at the time. Through their imperfections, you see the evolution of their greatest accomplishments play out within your own life.

Their generation started the uprising for love, peace, and freedom. They shook the designed structure made to contain and control them to experience something more fulfilling. They fought brutal wars, both social and political, so that you may enjoy the world you live in today. Vietnam, racial equality, women's liberation, alternative family constructs, religious freedom, rock 'n' roll, and protest filled the airwaves as they paved new ways of living counter culture to the "status quo" of their parents. Even though their visions of revolutionary change may not seem manifest in the current world drama, when they look into your eyes they know that not all has been lost. They beam with pride for all you have created and how you carry the torch of hope for a new day. They have nothing but support for you now, as you continue to rise to the next level of freedom and step lightly upon the earth. You honor your parents deeply and thank them for bringing you into this world.

Behind your parents, you see your grandparents. You respect the path that enabled them to bring your parents into the world. Wars, genocide, sacrifice, the Great Depression, and the Industrial Age consumed their existence. You observe that they had limited resources and fewer options available and feel their struggle. You honor your grandparents for their hardships, habits, and beliefs that molded your parents, and witness how these traits interweave into your own existence. If you met your grandparents, remember the times that you got to spend together and treasure the experience of worlds colliding. Can you see the world through their eyes when they were children?

Behind your grandparents, you see your great-grandparents. You may not know much about them, yet you feel their strength within you. They had their own challenges to survive—families left behind to escape wars of persecution, flights to the land of opportunity. They sacrificed everything to provide a better day for themselves and their children. They grew up in a different world, and would most likely have a hard time relating to the world you live in today. Without the distractions of technology or machines to do household chores, they spent most of their time and energy enduring the challenges of everyday existence. See the world through their eyes. What was it they desired beyond the limitation of their existence? Are there any common threads?

Behind your great-grandparents, you see a line of your great-great-grandparents. This lineage dates back to a century before your birth. Look through their eyes and experience the world they grew up in. Were they able to freely express themselves or did they have to disguise their longings for freedom of expression? Put yourself in their shoes to embrace their pain, suffering, joy, and celebration. As they grew their own food for their family, they had a harmonic connection with the earth. You bow to them for their perseverance through the cycles of seasons, enduring hardship yet planting their seeds for future generations.

Your great-great-great-grandparents are next. Although they express concern for you, they are not fully able to relate to your dilemma. This generation stands firm in reminding you of simplicity. They find you very brave to stand at the center of the storm, experiencing a kind of freedom they never knew existed. They worked hard to plant their hopes in the spring and reaped their harvest in the fall. They remind you to put your hands in the dirt and plant seeds that will feed you and future generations. You bow in gratitude for their courage.

Next to offer blessings are your great-great-great-great-grandparents, a generation one hundred and fifty years before your arrival that make up sixty-four people of your bloodline. They have come from all corners of the world to contribute to your gene pool. When you look into their eyes, you sense an essence of uprising within their way of life that unsettled the foundations upon which you now stand. They knew there was more to life than what they had been told. They sent their hopes and tears into the wind so that one day you might pick up their torch and continue to uphold the family line, putting their faith in better days ahead. You infuse their deepest longings into your quest.

As you look to the very last lines you can see with your naked eye, you see your great-great-great-great-great-grandparents. In their sight, you are the seventh generation. The veil is thin and you are able to cross barriers of time and space. You look deeply into their ancient wisdom and they smile. You realize the sacrifices and the leaps of faith they made in their own lives. Their world is so far removed, yet their tenacity helped bring you to this point. There is honor for the earth and the old ways that prevailed before modern life took its toll. You see both the harshness of their reality and the sparkle in their eyes as they embrace the simplicity of everyday life. There is contentment in the loving connection within the family unit and the strength of community that ignited their will to plant seeds for you, the seventh generation. No words are needed. You nod deeply into their souls with gratitude.

You see your lineage behind you, one hundred and eight total; each with their unique struggles, sacrifices, and victories. Each generation has been built upon the last; overcoming obstacles, refining dharma along the way. Their perseverance and endurance has brought you here. You can feel their support—the threads of character from all seven generations entwined into your present moment. You were their hope and their reason. Know that you are not alone and that you continue to carry the torch for all who came before you. You know you have the power to shift the foundation upon which future generations will stand. You honor your ancestors for bringing you to this point of change.

You have experienced seven generations, roughly 175 years into the past. Now it is time to witness the gifts of the future. Bring your awareness back to the present time as you hold a child close to you. Look into her eyes. You express unwavering hope for this child as she experiences the world. You teach her to care for the five elements, to act as a steward upon the earth, and to respect the diversity of others' beliefs within the human family. You explain above all else how important it is to revere the natural rhythms of the seasons, honor the directions, invoke sacred space, and share this knowledge as people stray further into technological and genetically modified advances. You warn this child not to give up in the face of adversity and overwhelming odds, and to remember to plant the seeds within and watch them grow. You encourage her to be the change she wishes to see in this world, the opportunity and the solution for a new day! See the world through the eyes of the next generation…

As time is fluid, witness your child growing into an adult. There is a new addition to your family lineage. Hold your grandchild in your arms, feel the kinship and the hope you have for this generation to flourish in sustainable, co-creative, and sovereign ways. See the world through his eyes. Again, you witness time speeding up and you watch your grandchild grow into a strong, courageous, and compassionate being driven by passion to care for the earth and unify the differences between people. You see the seeds of guardianship that you planted in your own child flourish in the next two generations.

Move on into the future to yet another addition to your family lineage. You hold your great-grandchild in your arms; you smell the freshness of his skin and the sweetness of his breath. This new life has sparked a walk down memory lane. You have been through many cycles of ebb and flow in your own experience and you have fully participated in the movements of transformation. You were a pioneer in your day for a new way of life. You fought for freedom in underground circles, infiltrating the matrix of control, and dismantled the structure by working within. You dreamed big, followed your bliss, and dared to evolve against all odds. Now you can barely recognize the world from when you were a child, as there have been many shifts to consider longevity and sustainability for future generations. And now, you hold your sweet great-grandchild with the ability to experience the world so many have helped to preserve. You plant the seed of stewardship into this future generation.

You are able to see your great-grandchild prosper before you make the journey from this life into the next. As you cross over, you experience what is beyond the implied vacuum of nothingness. You are still a full participant of life, witnessing your lineage unfold. You offer unconditional love and support to not only your bloodline but all of creation. You have become an ancestor; you hold space for your lineage and watch the seeds you have planted grow. Time is even more fluid and you watch your great-grandchild bring a child into the world. Again you sit in reverence as you witness what the new caretakers of the earth will inherit. You send your blessings further to the future to never give up hope and to continue to walk in grace with each step.

Next you see your great-great-grandchild grow up and walk with respect upon the earth. The new generation continues to hold the torch of stewardship. Your great-great-great-grandchild is born. The seeds continue to flourish from one generation to the next, giving hope, vision, purpose and focus for the greater good of all. You smile as you send your blessings on the wind. You see your great-great-great-grandchild compassionately serve the whole with impeccable humility. In time, a new life is added to your lineage. You see your great-great-great-great-grandchild born into the world of collective creation, the innocence and purity of new life unscathed by the tests of time. You send your blessings: may this generation remember to protect the earth, with a soft step and love in their hearts for each other and all of creation. You witness one more generation of your lineage… the seventh generation.

Your great-great-great-great-great-grandchild is born. Everything that you have worked for is present in this generation. You look into her eyes and she recognizes you as her ancestor. There is open communication between you, the ancient one, and your embodied hope. There are many questions asked about what happened back in your day, confirming written history. Not all facts are accurate, as they rarely are. You share your call to action during a time of deception and great upheaval. You explain that life is never easy, we are all here to learn and grow, yet when we heed the call to action to support the guardianship of the elements upon the earth, there is balance, peace, and love for all to blossom. You remind her to remember, to learn, to teach the ways to walk in harmony, and to continue to plant the seeds for the next generation. You send blessings from your vantage point behind the veil of perception, loving and supporting her through every facet of her existence! You ask her to carry the torch for she is the future for the next seven generations. You look through her eyes and you see the world you left behind. There is a heartfelt nod of recognition. You are complete and the cycle continues….

You look seven generations before your existence and look seven generations ahead at those who will come after you. Your family lineage is the roots of a tree expanding through you to the branches reaching for the sky; as above so below. You are reminded that you have chosen to be here at this time, you have chosen this lineage. You are no longer a victim of circumstance. You choose to take full responsibility and claim your place within your family line. In the present moment, you send a healing vibration through all the threads of your bloodline. Your family grid is whole and complete and weaves with other lineages throughout time to create a beautiful tapestry.

What is your contribution to your lineage? You realize that life is not about you, but about how you can serve the whole of existence. You look through your eyes from the vantage point of seven generations and see what is happening in the world around you. You see cracks in the system of control and domination, and the flaws in the global "American dream". You hear the cries of suffering of the five sacred elements. All of creation seeks a better way. You see past separation, embrace diversity, and clear the path for unity. You are the change and the hope for seven generations! What difference can you make in the world? What will you do today?

Active Journeys

Crossing the Bridge of No Return

After you jump into the fire of alchemy, you find yourself in canyon country. There is a long bridge that spans two canyon walls and a gatekeeper on both sides. There are fires and different groups at the edge of the cliff, and you are the guest of honor. Each fire has friends and family who have supported and challenged you along the way. As you go to each fire, be aware of the identity you present, the memories that resurface, the contracts, promises and pacts made, and any messages or parting words received. This may take you a while as there are many gathered around many fires to see you. Take as much time as you like. It is dark and you have until sunrise.

When the fires have turned to ash, all exchanges complete and emotions released, the sun begins to rise. It is a new day and you are free. You greet the sun and revitalize your strength through the solar codes you receive. You rededicate each step to the greater good of all. [5] When you have completed your communion with all of

---

[5] Refer to Aligning with the Ancient Rhythm page 25

existence, you look around you. Your tribe is standing and honoring the returning of the light with you. You feel the support of your soul family lift you up and give you extra courage to take the leap into the unknown. You take a moment to bow to them and send one last blessing before you turn your gaze back to the bridge spanning across the canyon. You make your way to the gatekeeper and humbly kneel before him. You ask his permission to enter the passage into the mystery. He looks into your eyes and peers into the depths of your soul. The silence following your request is heart wrenching, as you do not know how he will respond.

"You may pass but you must leave your identity behind as your fare to cross," he says. You realize the old images and definitions you have held for yourself no longer apply. You have learned that nothing is secure and nothing is guaranteed. Who you have been, what you have acquired, how you have acted and the relationships you have shared along the way are not who you are in this moment. You are ready to let go of the past, together with projections of how you thought things would be. You voluntarily strip yourself to the core essence of who you are. The gatekeeper directs, "Leave your personal belongings here, including your clothing, for other travelers who pass by. Put on this pilgrimage attire; you will stay warm and you will be recognized on the other side. Before you begin, you must cut your hair and renounce your vanity, as this will only get in the way of your refining process."

You do as you are instructed, leaving all that you had prepared to take with you, and purge the last of your identity. As you return to the mouth of the rope bridge, you feel renewed and lighter within your soul. You have birthed a new sense that is unrecognizable to your trained eyes. Again you humbly present yourself to the gatekeeper. "You may pass," he replies. "Once you begin this journey, there is no coming back as you will not be the same person who stands before me. May you have the courage to continue through your darkest moments, trust that you will have what you need, and stay focused. May you have many blessings on your journey."

With these final words, he hands you a simple knapsack with water, a few snacks, and a warm shawl. He steps out of the way and allows you to enter the crossing. You thank the gatekeeper for your initiation and do not look back. You take your first steps onto the rope bridge and it sways with your presence. You hold on to both sides for support as it steeply descends from the canyon wall into the ravine. You look out across the canyon to the other side, which seems so far away. You start to breathe deeply, take one step at a time, and practice mindfulness. The sun is shining, the birds are chirping, and you are carefree as you begin your undertaking across the chasm of destiny. You do not know what lies ahead, yet you know you will make it through. You dreamily take strides and create some distance from what you left behind. There is no going back now.

You start to see clouds build on the horizon; they are quickly heading your way. A gust of wind nearly knocks you off your feet and almost sends you spiraling to your demise. You hang on to the ropes as your life-line while the forces of nature pick up speed and toss you to and fro. You crouch down right where you are and hope you can trust in the fabric of your traverse. A blast of cool air chills you to the bone and you realize you are only a quarter of the way across the gorge. You grit your teeth and fight to take each step, continuing your journey onward.

The tempest continues to build momentum; there is no shelter to shield you from this storm. The wind intensifies its grip as it whips through every cell of your body. You realize that the harder you struggle the more its force is applied. And so you persevere through your inner turmoil and release your agenda of perceived comfort; instead of resisting, you relax your inner agitation to the external assault and find peace within. You continue to take one intentional step at a time, keeping your eyes carefully focused on the other side of the canyon. The whirlwind takes you to the edge of yourself and then suddenly ceases to care, and you are left raw to the core. The gusts have completely unraveled your equilibrium. Then you begin to feel droplets of rain. You have reached the midpoint of your voyage into the great unknown; the test of your character has just begun.

The rain starts slowly, it's a light sprinkle that moistens your skin and begins to dampen your clothing. Then the skies open up and the water pours down through everything you have left. The moisture has made the boards of the bridge very slippery and now you have a new task at hand. Staying upright is not only a challenge, it is nearly impossible. You decide to take off your shoes and put them in your knapsack so you have a better feel for what is beneath you as you slide perilously through each step. You can no longer see the other side of the canyon for the cloudburst has hidden your goal from sight. You rely on your inner compass. Slowly but surely you take one cautious step at a time. In your mind you begin to loop the questions: Would it be better to turn back? Will this be the end of me? Why am I here? Will I make it to the other side? Each of these questions and doubts takes you on a tangent far from the present moment. You observe how easy it is to distract yourself when things are uncomfortable; the challenge is not the storm, it is more personal. You strive to remain in the center and slice through the illusion of defeat.

You stop for a minute to collect yourself, pull the shawl from your knapsack, cover yourself with it and hunker down as the worst of the storm passes. As you wait out the monsoon, you are able to sink into a state of meditation, breathe, and receive guidance from your team. "You've got this! Don't give up!" the voices say. "Weathering this storm is part of your initiation. What awaits you is better than you can imagine. Have courage." These words give you some hope. Cold, wet, and distraught, you go into your inner darkness, rest there and accept your fate. From your inner caves, you begin to feel the warmth of your commitment return and you know that no matter what happens, you will make it through this. As you huddle under your protection from the elements and shiver, you hear a deafening crack—rocks breaking free from their resting place and plummeting into the abyss. This pounding puts your senses on high alert and your higher self shouts, "Move now!" There is no questioning this command. Collecting your bearings, you continue your journey through the torrential downpour.

The rain has let loose the flood gates. Waterfalls pour over the sides of the canyon walls, catapulting huge boulders. You continue your procession quickly, but suddenly there an explosion from where you came, and a red torch flashes through the sky above you. S.O.S. In a heartbeat, the bottom drops out of your foundation. You begin to fly through the air and drop into the crevasse. As your lifeline collapses around you, you catch a piece of rope that passes by. You hold on and weave yourself into the remains of the bridge as you speed toward the canyon wall. As the inevitable is within reach, you brace yourself for the oncoming impact. You slam into the rock with a velocity that nearly crushes your spirit. Dangling from your rope, you take quick inventory and realize you are OK—in one piece—sore from your collision. The hair on your neck begins to stand on end as an electric charge throws its fury through the sky. Bolts of lightning strike too close, shocking your composure. You feel defeated. You remember the snacks the gatekeeper put in the knapsack, which is miraculously still thrown over your shoulder. Wearily, you take a rest from the nightmare surrounding you and silently eat a bar of seeds.

After this temporary reprieve and nourishment, you take stock. You are dangling by a thread of ropes and boards, anchored into uncertainty. You decide to begin weaving your way up the canyon wall, first one arm, then the other, followed by each foot, all in perfect rhythm. You no longer panic about what could happen for the only path is up. This is a slow process. You struggle to keep your mind from bending into despair for you are determined it will not end this way. You hear, "Have faith, we are with you," and you know you are not alone. The rain begins to let up, and darkness follows suit. Raw and frayed from the twist of events on your journey across the canyon, you decide it is best to pause for the evening and continue your ascent when you can see your footing more clearly. You take some of the ropes of your lifeline and tie yourself into the bridge of your salvation. You wrap yourself in your shawl and completely relax all of your limbs, trusting the fibers to carry you through the night. Stars appear overhead, giving you hope that the storm has passed. You instantly fall into a deep sleep and are transported to a place beyond dreams. Before you awaken, you have a vision of the gatekeeper's intense gaze: "There is no turning back, this too shall pass," he says, looking deeply into your soul, yet this time there is a hint of a smile on his face which warms you to the core.

The chirping birds arrive in full glory and signal the dawn. You stir within the cocoon you made and notice how sore you are—but you are alive! —a survivor now rested and prepared to undertake the final leg of your journey out of the void. You are higher above the canyon floor than you thought and with the sunlight and clear skies on your side you are encouraged to continue on. Before you untangle yourself, you savor your last seed bar and drink from the canteen you carried all this way, remembering the eyes of your vision.

You are a believer. You have made it through a dark night of the soul. With gratitude, you pour some of your water on the earth below you and pray for safe passage to the other side. You repack your knapsack, put your shoes on, untether yourself from your lifeline, and begin the slow process toward the surface. You notice you are stronger this morning as you focus on each hand and foot placement. Ever closer to your destination, you breathe, drawing air into your center. You no longer have to attend to the demons of doubt and fear, as you are crystal clear and intent on the task at hand. The last pitch is within sight. Your lifeline is as tattered and worn as you are. Breathing and focusing your eyes on your mark, you reach the top of the canyon wall. As you pull yourself through your rite of passage, you feel an overwhelming sense of gratitude for your life and everything that has supported you against all odds. You drop to your knees, lift your hands to the sky, and praise the Creator for guiding and protecting you along the way.

There is no one to greet you and congratulate you on your feat. You stand alone, realizing the devastating damage the flash floods have done to the landscape. You also have been changed and molded by the forces of nature and tested to the very fiber of your being. Taking what little you have, you walk away from the edge of everything you have known and take a fresh step in a new direction. You head east without looking back.

Into the Labyrinth

Welcome to the "You"-curve ride! Hop aboard this tour that takes you deeper into yourself, shatters your projections, and creates an inspiring mosaic...a new You. The outcome may be unexpected. There are many twists and turns that will take you far away from where you thought you intended to be. Stay the course. Do not fear the trickery of the mind as the ego tries to control your response when the bottom drops out. Continue on your path even when you feel you have lost your way. There is only one way in and one way out; eventually you will reach the center of the labyrinth.

Note: The Labyrinth is a tool for a walking meditation; it is also a section on the Green River. You can change "steps" to "paddle strokes" to experience the water version of this meditation.

As you begin your journey, you are confident in who you are and know your place within the world. You know where you are going and have a good idea how to get there. Your vision is centered, success secured. Everything has brought you to this moment, trained you to focus and manifest your destiny, prepared you to endure the hardships along the way. As you enter the labyrinth, you leave familiar comforts and structure behind. You enter the unknown with an excitement that ignites your heart as you step with intention through the threshold of growth. The art of surrender is your compass in this territory of self-discovery. Your senses are alive and vibrant as you notice every detail surrounding you and stretch into an expression of yourself beyond your perception.

Your positive attitude initiates a positive experience. You are enjoying each moment in your adventure to the heart of deeper wisdom. Your goal is in sight and the flow is easy and forgiving. As you enter the first few bends your spirit soars at the beauty before you. Everything makes sense, including the placement of each footstep. As you round the next bend, thinking you are getting closer to your rite of passage, you discover that your path goes in the opposite direction. You wonder why the road is leading you away from your salvation, yet you continue to stay the course. Another bend in the trail sends your mind reeling into a "When will I get there?" attitude. You become impatient with the roundabout route.

You overcompensate your internal discord with an "everything will be fine" outlook, convincing yourself to return to the feelings you had when you started this journey. You think about all the people who have walked this path before you, not one of them mentioning an internal wobble of doubt. As you continue to the heart of the labyrinth, you start to question why you decided to embark upon this path in the first place. The trend of personal discovery and an "everyone is doing it" mentality has challenged you to join those who have had the courage to dig deeply into their human existence. The desire to follow through and take part in a mind-altering experience gives you the energy to carry on.

Further down the U-curve, your excitement stales and cracks begin to surface. As you continue around the next bend, only to find disillusionment where you thought promise was waiting, your spirit starts to plummet. With your goal nowhere in sight, you second-guess yourself and wonder if you made a wrong turn somewhere along the way. You become more disoriented with each step and decide to take a moment to regroup. You are lost. You begin to melt down and release the emotions propped up by false security and purpose. You lose your internal bearings and momentum; it is difficult to continue, for you are frozen within the canyons of your mind, trying to perceive order in the shattering of self unfolding. The aftershocks shake you to the core as you become more aware of your predicament. You can no longer keep it together. You lie down where your tears have begun to soak the earth and you pour your disenchantment into her folds. You roll around and pound your fists into the dirt to dispel your frustration and the terrorizing fear gnawing at your gut. Before long you are spent, raw, surprised by the intensity of your tantrum. This is not how you wanted things to be!

Coming back to yourself, you feel ridiculous that you fell apart in the middle of nowhere and consider turning back. From this vulnerable place you remember there is one way in and one way out. You resolve to continue to put one foot in front of the next and trust the process of the labyrinth. The further away you walk from the comforts of the past, the more present and aware you become. You align your steps with your breath, observe the ego's pull to madness, and claim your place within the elements. You are at the bottom of the You-curve. If you looked into a mirror, you might not recognize the image of who stands before the reflective surface on the edge of sanity.

What was true for you at the beginning of your journey, all your hopes and aspirations, no longer apply. You have outgrown the old concepts of fulfillment and prescribed boxes of happiness. Definitions of success and ambitious expectations loosen their hold as you soften your grip. Being in the valley, in the depths of the void, you plant the seeds of faith, not knowing where the path may lead. Accepting where you are and taking full responsibility for your experience, you begin to rise with a steady step. You realize that it is not about where you are going, or the end game, rather it's about how you show up in each moment. As you breathe consciously, aware of your body, mind, spirit connection, the walls climb higher as the mystery unfolds.

When you have just about given up on this quest and forgotten why you embarked on it in the first place, you round the next bend and suddenly arrive at the center of the labyrinth. There is nothing glorious about this place, yet you take a moment to take a deep breath. You sit in gratitude and experience inner peace as you let go of your personal agenda even more and open to divine will. You rest in this center devoid of striving to be something other than you are. Where you sit, the labyrinth has carved off the excess and illusion you have been fed since infancy. You are now free to access your full capacity and deepest truths. There is nowhere to go, nothing to be, just YOU. Rest easy and "be" for as long as you need to feel complete. It may take hours, it may take days. The stillness fills your coffers for the next leg of the journey.

From your center, you rediscover your connection to Source. Instead of searching for something outside of yourself for fulfillment, you reverse the polarity, and take in what you need. Through relaxing into serenity, your sense of purpose is revitalized. Your vision becomes clearer as you cultivate your poise. With intentional thought, you begin the process of manifestation while surrendering the outcome to the divine forces at play. Your magnetic presence opens the gates to receive the bounty of prosperity on all levels. This is the gift from the center of the labyrinth. This is one of the pleasant surprises that beckoned and encouraged you to venture inside the maze of emotion.

The center of the labyrinth is not the end of the journey, it is the midway point. You must exit the way you came. Fully restored by your new sense of self, you humbly take the steps back to where you started. Now you have a new vantage point as you slip through the bends in the path. The view is fresh from this angle and you no longer question your place within the labyrinth. You integrate each step with awareness as you round each bend with refreshed senses. You are not anxious where the path will lead nor do you feel the need to rush the process. You take one step at a time, fully present. Your mind is clear of debris of future plans and past misfortunes. The power of the Now guides you through the various perceived detours along the way. Before you know it, you have arrived at the beginning.

You are not the same "you" who entered the labyrinth a short while ago. Humbled, you look back from where you came and know that the journey is not about the destination so much as it is about every step along the way. Your misguided motivation of being part of the "enlightened" crowd has brought you to your knees to discover that your truth lies within. The steps of your journey are related to a much bigger picture. Instead of following the self-serving prophesy toward greatness, you see your service for the greater good of all.

You also realize the shortest distance between two points may be a straight line, yet the road less traveled refines the soul. When the road appears to lead no-where, this is where abundant treasures can be found. You had to let go of how you wanted things to be and the route you had planned to execute your goal to find the way to your center. The courage you called upon to face your shattering and voyage through a dark night of the soul has given you the strength to continue the jour-ney. You are spiraling up through cycles of deeper

"You-curve" learning. May you have faith above all else with each step you take.

Into the Flow

You have decided to venture onto the mighty Colorado River with some of your closest friends to test your courage on a paddleboard. When you arrive at the banks of the waterway, where you will begin your adventure, you meet your guide. She is a spunky rendition of Annie Oakley in a string bikini, braids and a trucker hat. She greets you with a pile of gear—a lifejacket, a paddle, a helmet, a leash, and an oversized board. Before she helps you into this bulky gear and begins her intro into paddleboarding, she has you sign your life away. The risks spelled out in black and white do not faze excitement; you sign on the dotted line without question. As your lifejacket is cinched beyond your lung capacity, you are reassured that this life saver will be your greatest friend of all time. Your guide goes over safety protocols, paddle stroking, board orientation, then explains that the river has many temperaments, especially with the 20,000 cfs (cubic feet per second) raging past the shore.

She tells you that there are smooth glassy sections that invoke care-free drifting where the water glides effortlessly downstream. There are eddies which take the unassuming rookie back upstream, and the unforgiving eddy line where the two currents meet. There are also sections of the river where chaos reigns— when the water passes over and through an obstacle and a mighty rapid is formed. The guide shares her theory about successfully maneuvering through a rapid. 25% is entry, 25% is skill, 25% is the river's will, and 25% is luck. In her mind, there is a 50/50 chance of making it through a rapid unscathed. With these odds, you fret about the terrifying and exhilarating experience of addressing these roaring monsters that await you downstream. Ms. Oakley instructs you to execute a 45 degree angle to ferry across the current, choose your entry into the rapid, keep your craft straight when the waves surge with the flow, and keep faith in your paddle stroke. Then her eyes glow with passion as she reminds you to never give up even when you think you have been beaten. She assures you that the last push of water may release you from the grips of defeat. With that she lets you loose in a recirculating eddy to apply the tips of engagement.

As you enter the flow and attempt to stand on your board, you realize it is a little shakier than you had antic-ipated. Your legs find a new balance, using muscles you have never engaged before, dealing with the unstable environment of the water swirling around you. You hear your guide cautioning you to keep your paddle in the water at all times, and this helps steady your teetering confidence. Your flailing paddle keeps you upright one second, while the next you are submerged in an icy cold embrace. The startling chill takes your breath away as your lifeline floats you near your board, which is dancing upon the surface. With your paddle in one hand, you reach toward the handle and attempt to pull yourself up on your board. There is nothing graceful about this maneuver as you grip, pull, push, kick, slither your way out of the water, and flop your extremities back onto your craft. Drenched to your core you humbly acclimate to the flow. Your guide decides you are all ready to start the adventure downstream. You do not know what is in store as you embark upon this journey, but you keep an open mind and zest for the unfamiliar.

Your guide explains that around the next bend is the first riffle you will encounter on your voyage. She recommends dropping to your knees though the first set of rapids and hitting the waves straight with the bow of your board. You are filled with anticipation and question your ability to make it through the raging waters. She encourages you to continue breathing as the speed of the river accelerates faster than the heart pounding in your chest. The roar becomes more deafening than a freight train; frothy water drenches and consumes your board from every direction, and time slows down. You keep your eyes on the rising waves before you and brace your paddle to keep you upright. In a matter of seconds, you have made it through to the other side still right side up and let out a holler in celebration. You gather with your fellow comrades to share tales of the wild ride, wide grins all around.

You have a moment of reprieve as you regain your feet beneath you and relax into the flow. The water is smooth sailing as it careens down multiple bends in the river. You are able to counteract the various boils and whirlpools filling deep voids within the depths of the channel through which you float. You are skimming the surface with effortless paddle strokes as you engage your core with the flow. The beauty surrounding you polishes your character as it has done for eons of time. The canyon walls etch their history, the blue heron follows you to the next rock just out of reach, the water churns, other birds sing, and the wind begins to whisper sweet nothings into your face. Everything seems right in the world as you commune with your environment and become one with the flow. You have found your groove, relaxing into the swift volume of moving water with ease and grace.

As you round the next bend those sweet nothings turn into a ferocious blast. The wind raises its fury to let her presence be known. There is no use cursing the gusts that slice through your bones. Now it is time to stand and face the depths of your grit. You put your head down, keep your paddle in the water, and continue to pick your way downstream. The wind's force blows you back upstream, making each motion vital to attain forward momentum. You make peace with the elements as you unify your force with nature, one paddle stroke at a time. The up-canyon breeze nearly knocks you off your board as it turns you sideways. You return to your knees and per your guide's bellows, stab your paddle in the water so the current can assist with your progression. You relax into submission as you wait out the assault and continue downstream against all odds. In good time, the wind lets up and releases the pressure within your mind.

Annie collects your group and explains that the next feature is one of the bigger challenges on this section of the river. She says, "Some stop and scout the rapid, tentatively plotting a course of action only to have the best laid plans change mid-rapid; others read and run the river. Either way, there is a state of mind one must achieve to face what is downstream. There is a "Zen moment" where the mind becomes a blank slate and melts into the flow, leaving one's destiny up to fate." With that your guide fearlessly takes on the raging wild. Now you are ready for the seething torrents below you. You are standing up as you enter the first wave, breathing with each paddle stroke. You are beyond fear of the unknown, fully present with the curling waves ahead while the adrenaline pumps through your veins. In the heat of battle, your board jigs while you jag right into the water at the base of a wave. You are sent to the bottom of the river before you resurface to take a full breath of life-giving oxygen. In the midst of the chaos, you remember to keep your feet downstream and your paddle in your hand as you collect your composure. When you grab for your board it turns over, making it near impossible to get back on. You resist the struggle, relax into your fate, and bob through the peaks and valleys of the wave train.

Toward the end of your scuffle with the flow, the current presents an eddy, making it possible to escape the grip of its wet talons. You are able to finally swim to the handle on one side and flip your craft upright, then pull yourself back onto your board. The mighty Colorado has humbled you and brought you to your knees; you take deep breaths to make up for the loss of air within its cooling kiss. Waterlogged and chilled to the bone you take a moment to lie on your board and reset your resolve. You now know the power and the strength of the river first hand. Given your close encounter with this unharnessed force of nature, you give thanks to the Creator for being able to live another day. The sun shines upon your face and warms the wet layers of your body, mind, and spirit.

Your guide comes over and asks if you are okay. Even though you have been shaken to your core, you have never felt better. You feel alive. The water has a way of cleansing the overzealous spirit into an awe-inspired awakening. The river is much bigger than you can conceive and you are a minute particle witnessing its power. You realize there is no taming this beast or getting a handle on properly picking your line through it; you leave mastery for another day. The more you surrender your agenda beyond all thought, the more you find a zone where humility and full participation meet. You have learned about going with the flow. You return a smile to your guide, tapping the top of your head in response to her question, and continue downstream.

When you look at your friends, you realize that the river has changed you all. Some are wide-eyed, some quiet, some are soaked and grinning from ear to ear, yet all understand the power of the Colorado. This tributary has woven tighter bonds among you and your comrades as the shared experiences of drifting and surfing sheer chaos replays in your minds. Laughter and words of encouragement fill the air as everyone recounts their journey through the river's jaws of death. Past a few more bends downriver, your guide points to a beach on the bank and you follow her lead. You cross the flow and enter the calm eddy on the other side, and discover that you have reached your destination and are safely back on dry land. As you disembark from your first voyage, you detach your leash, pull your board onto the beach, your paddle in hand, and raise your voice in gratitude to the canyon walls. As you celebrate victory with your friends you give your guide a big lifejacket hug. The river has not been conquered, it can never be conquered! But you have survived its many temperaments and found a new passion along the way.

A Prayer

May we humbly bow to the Creator of all that is and may all of creation be our witness. We are here; listen to our call.

Let us pray for the broken heart within the human condition. The suffering is not outside of ourselves; we observe the discord within and see it all around us. May we feel the longing for unconditional love within a world of conditions and compartments of what is acceptable and what is divergent. May we radiate pure LOVE and soothe the pain that no longer serves us. May we see each other as a reflection of the Source and learn to love each other deeply. Within the darkness of separation, destruction, and powerlessness let us pray for unity, as we are all interconnected. We are powerful beyond measure; when we support one another we empower the whole. We are in this together. We are ONE.

Let us pray to discover the peace within and drink deeply from this well so we may experience peace on Earth. May peace within our minds and hearts create stillness within the chaos. Beyond constant ambition, striving and distraction lies the fullness of the moment. Let us open space to rest from the battle and breathe deeply into the NOW. May we remember this practice daily; our vigilance is our torch and helps us pierce through the veils of illusion with the clarity of sight.

Let us pray to humbly put our egos aside and learn what we are here to master in this lifetime. May we look within for the answers to our own truths and share them with those who are ready to listen. We each have our own unique gifts and inspirations to bring to the whole. Let us take full responsibility for our actions and personal growth so we may integrate our piece into the collective vision. May we flourish with infinite prosperity on all levels as we add self-discovery to all of creation. We are co-creators of life beyond constraint toward the highest frequencies of love and freedom. May we shine our light without fear and contribute to the evolution of the high vibration on Earth.

Let us pray for the courage to endure these times of challenge. Pressure creates the finest diamonds and fire creates the toughest steel. May we continue to stay the course, participate with our full presence, remain focused with our purpose at this time, and celebrate the opportunity to grow. We have chosen to be here and we volunteered for this great transition. May we have faith, trust, and belief in the process, knowing that we are fully supported by all that is, and transcend struggle to learn our greatest strengths. Let us bring hope into the darkest spaces both within ourselves and the external hologram.

Let us give voice to those that do not have one. Let us pray for the earth, the animals, the waters, the minerals, the plants, and the children. May we give back to all that provides us with sustenance and protect these resources, as our future depends on it. May we integrate sustainable living into our daily tasks as we directly impact seven generations. Let us pray for the longevity of all life.

May we live in gratitude for this opportunity to connect and share our truth. May our prayers ripple through the matrix and peacefully facilitate shifts within the structure of control. May our movement of reformation propel us into the next era of completion. We are the change we want to see in the world. We are here. Listen to our call. It is done. It is done. It is done.

Notes:

Epilogue

Inner Sol Alchemy Self-Discovery Guide

Step 1: Recognize habits, addictions, beliefs, stories, blocks, excuses, distractions, thoughts, relationships, and reactions that no longer serve your greater good and highest potential. Making peace and forgiving how we got to this point in our journey is the first step to recovery. We must accept ourselves completely where we are or we may have to repeat our self-destructive patterns over and over again. It is far easier to accept our wholeness, fullness, and glory than to humbly accept our broken, wounded, destitute selves. In order for anything to change, we must be able to look into the mirror and remember our truth. We must see past our dysfunction without judgment and reclaim our self-love and self-worth in order to begin this journey.

Step 2: When we hit the wall within ourselves and reach the breaking point, we get to choose a new way of being, reaction, and response. There is a point where enough is enough and there has to be another way. Ganesha is the Indian deity with an elephant head who is known to remove obstacles when invoked. I recently heard a revised version of Ganesha's gift: He does not remove the obstacles for you; rather he guides you through the obstacles within yourself. When we are able to honor an obstacle as a gift of learning and growth and enter a state of allowing and acceptance, we begin to open to new possibilities and continue through to the other side. Where there is resistance, our patterns will persist. With every breakdown there is a breakthrough. It is important to want something different for yourself and be willing to follow through with the commitment to grow in a new way. No one can decide for you that it is time to make a change. Only when you are ready will this process work for you to discover your highest potential! The journey of self-discovery is not for the faint of heart. No half-stepping, no half-hearted commitments or maybes may enter here. Full presence is required.

Step 3: Set up a support system. Let friends and family know of your new decision in your life. This will not only give you accountability, but will also provide a good network to connect to when times get tough. There will be good days and there will be bad days at the beginning of any major change or shift. Reaching out to someone who makes you feel safe and supported is paramount to recovery. Sometimes old friends will drop away, as they no longer resonate with your new state of being. There may be times when you choose to isolate yourself. This is fine as long as there is a balance. There are times to lick our wounds so they may heal. Know you are never alone and that many have walked this path before you.

Inner Sol Alchemy has created an online gathering once a week to support those who are committed to the process of self-mastery and connect to others on the path. As a partner in the self-discovery program, I am also committed to be a mentor for your process. Feel free to contact me at any time to work through what you are feeling during this road to recovery and self-realization: soljourneysretreat@gmail.com.

Step 4: Parting ceremony: death of the old. Honor the part "____" has played in your life, and find gratitude for getting you to this point within yourself. We let go of our old patterns and grieve the loss. When we take the time to purify, empty, and free ourselves of deep-rooted suffering, we open to rebirthing a new identity without "____" in our lives. This may be a quick or a lengthy process. Take your time and do not skip this step! Perform whatever death ritual feels right. A possible parting ritual may look like: lighting a candle, reciting a poem or writing a letter to what you are ready to let go of. Then burn it. After, write a letter to yourself about what your life will be like without "____" holding you back. CONGRATULATIONS! This is your new RE-BIRTH day! As with a celebration of life, it is time to celebrate you!

Step 5: We are creators of our reality. What we believe, think, say, and visualize creates the structure in which our reality unfolds. We invite our experiences to us. Let us take full responsibility for this power and be vigilant with our self-talk. It is easy to repeat familiar ways of being and expressing ourselves that will perpetuate our current experiences. In order to make changes, begin to observe yourself. Embrace a new I AM experience. Instead of professing to be an addict of any sort, we are going to reclaim our I AM presence. I am reborn. I am empowered. I am capable. I am strong. I am inspired. I am all possibilities. I am pure potential. I am valued. I am connected. I am loved. I am worthy! I am part of the collective. In times of weakness or emptiness, repeat these affirmations and mantras to refill and re-inspire yourself. Let these statements be our feathers for flight as we enter into the void within ourselves.

Step 6: Humbly bow to the Source to fill us with courage as we go deeper into ourselves. Ask for help from our guides to assist us when we get triggered and have the urge to go back to old familiar patterns that have given comfort in the past. We have a team that will assist us when we ask. Ask for guidance and you shall receive; this is a universal law. We are rarely taught how to listen or recognize the signs that there are bigger presences in our lives that not only protect us and help us in times of need, but also help align us with our new perceptions. Humbly reach out, they are waiting. It is important to step out of our humanness in order to open space for Spirit and our higher self to take center stage. Trust and have faith that the realms of benevolent, creative, unconditional love have your greatest good at heart.

Step 7: Discover our core wound, lean into the pain. Once we have removed our old patterns, let us explore the core wound that we have been numbing with our favorite sensory overload. As humans, we have been addicted to an old perception of the physical. Within our cellular memory we remember the great separation from our oneness. This fragmentation may show up as unworthiness, conditional love, co-dependence, manipulation, shame, guilt, sadness, anger, or fear. The experience of duality has manifested as disease in every possible way since the beginning of time. NOW we can choose to collect all of our past energy, heal our dis-ease, and reclaim re-integration within ourselves as well as with each other. We no longer have to replay the age-old dilemmas of the disempowered feminine or the masculine warrior unable to access his emotional side while preparing and executing war. We are rewriting and rewiring our patterns along with potential outcomes. First we must let go of being victims of circumstance, accept our lessons in this life—as we have signed up for them—and ultimately reclaim our power. Recognize how this core wound has shown up for you and how you have fed it up until this moment. It is time to heal ourselves! Call in love to enter your body and assist in letting go of all that no longer serves you.

I highly recommend making appointments with an energy medicine practitioner, a massage therapist, or acupuncturist to help rebalance and realign your energy system to facilitate deeper healing. As part of this program you also will receive a hands-on or distance healing from me, please call to schedule an appointment.

Step 8: Our reality as we experience it daily (our outer world) is a direct reflection of our relationship to ourselves. We have heard countless times from the mystics that life is an inner journey. If things are not working in the outer expression of our lives, then instead of blaming someone, let us take full responsibility for our experiences. Let us find the solutions and peace by the journey into ourselves. Let us enter the void, embrace fundamental groundless-ness, and meet our shadows. The darkness within ourselves holds great wisdom. Instead of running away from ourselves and filling the void with endless pleasures and desires, we begin to sit and listen to our needs and the parts of us that wish to be heard.

When we take stock of our inner chalice, are we leaking out our vital life force energy? Is our cup full, half full, or empty? Do we need to empty in order to repair? How are we filling ourselves from the inside? When we learn to fill ourselves up and give to others from the overflow of our cup, we may access the infinite abundance of energy.

Step 9: Creating new rituals: As with any change, it is best to replace old habits with new healthy habits. Do any or all of these rituals upon waking or before bed to bring the sacred path of self-mastery into your life.

*Gratitude: Give thanks for everything that is in your life. This is a great tool to recognize all the gifts we have received as well as step out of lack and struggle.

*Connecting to Source: When we tap into infinite energy, we claim our space with our full presence.

*Listening to guidance: Open to communication from our higher self—receive answers and direction for the questions we have inside.

*Heart Space Temple: When we live from our hearts, our world changes. The temple within our hearts is a place of self-exploration and deep meditative practices.

*Shield: Let us create a sacred space to maneuver in this world in which we honor ourselves and protect our energy. We no longer have to engage in war or have to explain our perspectives and truths of a new way of being. We no longer need external validation nor are we affected by external circumstances.

Step 10: Where do we go from here? We are a revolution of the mind, body and spirit! When we choose to be free from what no longer serves us, we awaken to our true potential. Let us understand our new vibration and the vibration of the world in which we live. Let us see the bigger picture outside of our own drama and process. May we have deep unconditional love and compassion to see past the illusion. It is time to realize that the evolution of mankind has played its part perfectly and we no longer have to perpetuate what has befallen humanity. We have asked to be here at this time and we are an essential piece to the whole. When we take off the shackles of limitation that we have placed upon ourselves as well as heal ourselves from the collective wound of separation, we become whole and we can become of service to humanity.

We can give back and contribute our gifts to the whole. What is our purpose? We can choose to be in the NOW moment rather than stuck in the past or living in the future. From pure presence, we can create what is beyond limits. How we paint this new canvas is up to us. How will we create our new foundation? What will we bring forth? How will we expand beyond all limitations into our full expression of potential and human being-ness? When you open a door, all possibilities will meet you there. What would someone who loves themselves do? The answers to these questions will open a life of inspiration. This is an exciting dance! Let us be ecstatic with this unfolding! Awaken to your magnificence! The chief attribute of self-mastery is silence. You have an internal knowingness and are wise beyond words. Feel who you are!

Step 11: Staying inspired. I find that listening to inspirational videos and discussions allows me to connect to the bigger picture. There are so many inspired beings who can guide us along the way. Much like peeling the onion, this process has many layers to reveal, explore and expand. Use the tools that work best for you.

Notes:

Acknowledgments:

Writing this first body of work has stretched me beyond all aspects of myself and through this process I have changed. At times I have lost both my perspective and foundation upon which some of these concepts were built, resulting in revision upon revision in order to uphold my responsibility to truth. As I have overhauled myself and Sol Journeys, I have received much encouragement and support along the way. I am so grateful for my family and my friends who have risen to this occasion. Thank you all for your input and comments that have helped Sol Journeys become what it is today. I am also grateful for all of the teachers who have helped shape who I am and brought me to this moment. For the skill of leadership and commitment, I value the insight and tenacity of my sisters. For pushing me beyond the constructs of my beliefs and motives while opening my eyes to the bigger picture, I thank Elisa. A special thanks goes out to my mother for assisting me with the art of the written word. I have an appreciation beyond words for the hours and dedication of my editor, Nancy Kurtz—for helping my literary expressions make sense and for keeping my motivation in check, from the deepest place within my heart I thank you for sharing your experience and wisdom! I know this is only the beginning. As I launch Sol Journeys into the world of publishing, I open to the FLOW...

About the Author

Alicia Wright is a visionary and a creative spirit. She is passionate about her service of liberation through awareness and facilitates empowerment through tools of introspection and connection. As an artist and a mother, she has learned the valuable tools of patience and perseverance. Alicia is a second degree black belt in Tae Kwan Do and teacher of practical self-defense for many years. Since 2008 she has owned and operated Bella Sol Spa, an energetic esthetic business, where she helps those who seek to find beauty on the inside. In 2015 she launched Sol Journeys: a guided retreat experience in tandem with this collection of journeys. Alicia was born and raised in Steamboat Springs, Colorado and in 2013 moved to Moab, Utah, to start anew as a business owner, desert explorer, truth seeker and paddle board guide on the Colorado River.

57790578R00100

Made in the USA
Charleston, SC
22 June 2016